An Island Childhood

growing up on Rathlin Island

by Augustine McCurdy

Published 2010
© Augustine McCurdy

ISBN: 978 1 906689 25 4

Printed by:
Impact Printing

Foreword

Over the decades there have been considerable changes on Rathlin. Our self-sufficient way of life has gone and we have joined the consumer society. Everything is bought in, including basics such as milk and bread. There is no more milking of cows and very little bread is home baked.

We have modern ferries, both fast and slow, and vehicles can come in and go out at will. Heating oil or coal is now delivered to the door and all we have to do is pay for it. No more cutting of peat or sods off the hill, or heaving bags of coal in and out of an open boat and on to a cart. Electricity now comes in via an undersea cable from Ballycastle and bottled gas is available on the island.

There is no more arable farming and no cultivating of fields. Many of the former fields are being taken over by briars and there is very little growing of vegetables or potatoes. Herds of cattle or flocks of sheep now graze the fields and hills and the only crop is grass which is cut in the summer, and wrapped up in black plastic for winter feeding of cattle There are plenty of large tractors to do this work and if a machine cannot do it then it does not get done, a spade is becoming a rarity.

What has been lost? The evening ceili has gone as people now spend their time watching TV, most of which has no relevance to daily life on Rathlin. The informal unannounced visit has gone as has the helping hand when needed. Most of all the population has declined from 250 to around 100 and young people cannot afford to buy a house as developers' holiday houses have pushed the price well beyond their reach.

Finally, despite these changes, Rathlin is still a good place to live. There is no crime and it is a good place for children to grow up where there is an excellent primary school even if the numbers are small.

Augustine McCurdy

Contents

Photographs

Other Books By the Author

Rathlin's Rugged Story
Walking on Rathlin
Stories and Legends of Rathlin
A History of Rathlin Irish

The Early Years

July 11 1930 was a significant day for me. It was the day I arrived into this world at Dalriada Hospital, Ballycastle, and within a few days, my mother and father brought me on the mail boat to Rathlin Island, and then two miles by horse and trap to my parental home.

This was the farm where my father's people had lived since 1850, having previously lived in the townland of Kebble at the western end of the island. The landlord of the time decided to turn it into a sheep ranch, and so all the tenants were moved to other holdings. This was achieved by dividing up existing tenancies into smaller lots, much the same process as had been carried out in Scotland during "the Highland Clearances" of the 1740s.

My father had spent his childhood days in this stone-built, thatched and whitewashed house, and attended the Rathlin public elementary school. In 1908, at the age of twelve, he was awarded a scholarship by the Gaelic League to attend Cloughaneely College, Gortahork, in Donegal.

During his three years of study there, he and the other students boarded with local families at a cost of 10 shillings (50p) per week for full board. It was the policy of the Gaelic League to spread the benefit of this around the local area, which with its small tenant farmers, was similar to Rathlin in many ways.

He studied the Irish language and history, qualifying as an Irish language teacher, however, on completion of his studies, he chose to take another road, contrary to his mother's expectations. He went instead to Greenock in Scotland, where he had three uncles living.

My mother Kathleen, was from Belfast, but she made an early acquaintance with Rathlin. Her father, Sean McNearney, came to Rathlin in 1912, as foreman on the construction of the West Lighthouse, bringing his family with him. This was a difficult contract, and they lived in a wooden company house near the

Joseph McCurdy, my grandfather, taken at James McCurdy's house, South Cleggan, c. 1900

Johny Coyle's Mail Boat leaving Rathlin 1922
Courtesy of Ian McLean

My parents on their wedding day, 1929
l. to r.: My aunt, Mary Margaret McCurdy, Paddy Black "red"
Ballygill, Clare Anderson, Post Office, Mickey Joe Anderson,
Glackanacre, Tessie Black, Glacklugh, my father Augustine
McCurdy, my mother Kathleen nee McNearney,
Mary Anderson Post Office.

Isabella McCurdy, Cleggan,
Elizabeth McCurdy,
Garvagh (my aunt)
c.1914 Belfast.

top of the cliffs at Cooraghy, where a jetty and inclined railway were constructed to bring building materials in by sea.

For my mother and her sister and brother, the three-mile walk to school on Rathlin every day was a dramatic change from walking a few hundred yards to school in the city.

When the lighthouse contract was completed they all returned to Belfast, although my grandfather went on to another contract on the construction of the Silent Valley Reservoir in the Mourne Mountains.

My mother continued her schooling in the city, later taking a job in Woolworths store in High Street in the city centre.

In the 1920s my father, having been in the British army during the First World War, went to work in Belfast, where he remained for eight years, when he returned to his island home, to look after his father, who was getting frail, his mother was deceased.

During his years in Belfast, he met up with my mother, whom he had known briefly on Rathlin when she had come   with her parents.

The friendship with my father developed, and so in 1929 she returned to Rathlin, where they were married.

It was a considerable change for both of them. For my father, settling down to a farming routine after being away for so long, was a challenge.

For my mother, it was equally challenging, exchanging a steady job and the amenities and social life of the city, for farm life on an island, which was dependent on fishing boats to maintain a link with the outside world. There was no public transport, no trams nor buses, so that walking everywhere was the only option. The two shops, the Church, harbour and school were all a two-mile walk on gravel roads full of potholes.

Milking cows, baking bread, churning milk for butter and many other jobs were all new to my mother, but she soon adapted. Having lived for a few years on the island as a child was a help.

Our House

Our house was built in the lee of a hill for shelter, like most of the older houses on the island, and ran in an east/west direction, in keeping with the tradition of Christian Churches, and so the sun was always on the front of the house.

The barley straw, used for thatching, was grown on the farm, it was held in place by wire netting stretched tightly across the roof, and tied to pegs along the sides and gables, this protected the thatch against westerly gales. The walls were whitewashed with lime, which could be obtained at the Rue Lighthouse, as it was a by-product of the acetylene gas which provided the light at that time. I can remember going with my father and the horse and cart to the Lighthouse for a load of lime. When it was mixed with warm water and with a bluebag added, it made good whitewash.

The interior was laid out like most of the old houses, there was a good sized entrance porch, where milk and buckets of water were kept on a stand, this led into a large kitchen which had a small bedroom off, as well as a half loft with wooden steps leading up to it. This served as storage space or extra sleeping space if needed. Then there was the main bedroom where my parents slept, as well as my brother and myself, it had a small fireplace where my father would light a fire on cold winter nights. I always remember the beds with curtains and valances around them to keep out draughts, the floor was covered in green patterned linoleum.

The kitchen was the heart of the house, all the cooking was done on the open fire, meals were taken at a large farmhouse table covered in white oilcloth. There was a dresser where all the crockery was kept on shelves, with cooking pots stored in a cupboard underneath, the churn stood in a corner where it was handy on churning day.

At night we sat around the fire, which had an armchair on each side, where my parents sat, also six other chairs around the table, as well as a form or long bench, if visitors came in they would pull a chair out from the table, or if cards were to be played, they sat around the table. I also did my homework at the table. Sacks of meal and flour were kept on a bench along the wall, the heat from the fire kept them dry, so life revolved around the kitchen.

The name of our house and farm was 'Garvagh', which translates from the Gaelic to 'rough field'. It consisted of forty-eight acres, including fifteen acres of arable land and the rest was rough grazing. Part of this rough grazing, known as Pairc Mor, was held in common with our neighbours, the Blacks of Glacklugh. By arrangement we grazed the cattle at different times of the year, so that they wouldn't be mixed up.

The land was a light loam, better than some farms, but was not so good as others. There were some families on the island who had no farm but had just enough ground to grow some potatoes and vegetables. There was a spring well nearby, and all the water for the house was carried in white enamel buckets from this well.

We had a horse called Molly, also cows, sheep, a goat, hens and ducks, as well as a collie dog called Brian, and a cat called Blackie.

My early years passed very pleasantly. When I was learning to walk, I used Brian, the dog, as my support, pulling myself up by holding on to the hair on his back. He was a very good-natured dog, having led a peaceful life until my arrival. He and the cat Blackie spent a good part of their lives sleeping in the straw in the barn.

Brian's work consisted mainly of herding the cattle from one field to another. In the evening he would go on his own and fetch the cows into the byre. He only had to be told to get the cows, and off he would go. His other main job was keeping the hens out of the vegetable garden, where they could very quickly wreak havoc on the young plants.

I would run after the hens and pester them, although I was kept well away from the larger livestock.

Blackie, the cat, tolerated me, even though I sometimes pulled his tail. His main role was to keep the mice in check as they were always in the stacks of corn in the stackyard.

Molly, the horse, did all the heavy work, ploughing in the springtime, harrowing the fields after the corn and barley were sown, making drills for planting potatoes, as well as all of the carting. She would get a rest in the summer, and graze the new grass and kick her heels. In some years my father would cut hay, and a summer job for Molly would be carting it into the stackyard.

Household Jobs

My mother baked bread on the griddle, every other day, over an open fire. The fireplace had an iron crane fixed in one corner, which could be swung out to hang a pot or griddle on the crook. This was hooked on to the crane with a short length of chain. The pot or griddle could be raised or lowered with the crook.

White flour, which my father brought from Ballycastle in ten-stone bags, was used for baking bread. My mother would put a couple of scoops of flour into a large crockery bowl, add a teaspoon of baking soda and a teaspoon of salt and mix it all together dry, then, adding buttermilk she would mix it to a pliable dough with her hands. Lifting it on to a floured breadboard, she would knead it well before rolling it out flat to about an inch thickness. After cutting it into five or six triangular shaped farls it was ready for the griddle, and she would then sprinkle some flour on the griddle. If this flour turned brown the griddle was hot enough, and she would put the farls on it to bake. If more heat was needed she would throw a handful of heather or whins (gorse) on the fire for a quick blaze. After seven or eight minutes the farls were ready for turning over.

The bread would be baked in about twenty minutes, and often I would get a piece spread with butter. There is no taste on earth to equal warm freshly-baked bread and butter.

Other types of bread were made by adding either barley meal, yellow meal (ground maize) or oaten meal. Once or twice a week my mother would also make potato bread or 'fadge' as well as pancakes. She would sometimes add a handful of currants or raisins to the white bread as a treat.

The oven pot was brought into use for baking a cake. It was set directly on the fire, and hot coals piled around and on top of it. It would be done in a couple of hours. The oven pot was also a great way to roast a chicken.

The barley and oats grown on our own farm were ground in the mill in Ballycastle. My father would send a few bags of each to the mill. The oats were great for making porridge and the hens were also given a handful or two to keep them laying in the winter.

Another chore was churning, which my mother would do once a week. The cream was skimmed off the milk daily and put into a large earthenware crock, where it would turn sour. On churning day, it was poured into the upright wooden churn, and after twenty minutes or so of steady work with the churn staff, grains of butter would begin to form. At this stage a drop of cold water was added, which helped to gather the butter together into a solid lump. Then it could be lifted out into an enamel basin, where it was worked with wooden butter spades and cold water.

When all the buttermilk was removed it was ready for making into small blocks of about one pound, or sometimes shaped with round wooden butter prints. These would have various patterns cut into them, such as grains of corn or a swan. The buttermilk was saved and made a very refreshing drink and it was also used for baking.

In the winter, churning was more difficult due to colder weather, but to counteract this the churn would be stood near the fire, or sometimes boiling water was added. Too much of this would produce scalded butter, which was very pale in colour.

There was no piped water in Rathlin houses in those times. Water had to be carried from a spring well in enamel buckets, which were kept for this purpose. Our well was close to the house and was a natural spring, so it never went dry. It was always icy cold, and a couple of buckets of water would last all day,

On washday, my father would carry five or six buckets buckets of water from the well, and pour it into a wooden barrel, where my mother could get it for the washing. She would first boil up some water in the large kettle, and then soak clothes in a tin bath with hot water and a soap powder called Rinso. After a while she would lift them out and scrub them on a washboard, using a bar of Sunlight soap. My father's dungarees which he wore at the lighthouse, were often covered in oil or paraffin and so they would first have to be boiled in a zinc bucket before rinsing out. All the clothes were then hung out on a line to dry, making sure that the cows could not get at them. I remember my mother putting sheets out on the grass to bleach, when one of the cows came along and started chewing at them. They will chew anything when searching for salts or minerals.

Of course washing in the wintertime was more difficult, it was not easy to dry clothes outside, so they were hung on lines across the kitchen, to dry by the heat of the fire, every time you walked in you would get a faceful of wet washing.

The day would start with breakfast, which we would have after the cows were milked and fed. It usually consisted of porridge made in a small three-legged pot from our own ground oats, with milk and water mixed.

When it was ready, my mother would put it into deep white bowls, adding fresh milk straight from the cow, as well as a spoonful of sugar. Sometimes I would put some more in when she wasn't looking.

After breakfast, the day's work would begin. Feeding the calves with a bucket of fresh milk was the first chore. In the winter there was no field work so my father would thresh some straw for feeding the cows and any other young cattle

Threshing was done with a flail, which consisted of a hand-staff and a souple. The hand-staff was made of any hardwood available, such as ash and the souple was made of hazel. These woods were obtained from the mainland around Glenshesk. Both souple and handstaff had a shallow groove cut around them a couple of inches from the top, and the binding was a strip of sheepskin or soft upper leather lapped two or three times around both. The loose end was then tucked into the laps, not tied in a knot.

The grain from threshing was stored in sacks in the barn, where the cat slept. It was her job to keep mice away from the grain, which was next year's seed.

The cows were well looked after. On very cold days they would stay in the byre for most of the day, except for a run out for an hour or two for a drink of water. They would have turnips and corn to eat as well as straw, and were provided with a straw bed.

My father would do the milking about six o'clock in the evening by the light of a storm lantern, and the cows and horse would get their last feed about nine o'clock in the winter, when the lantern was lit again. It burned paraffin and the wick had to be trimmed regularly or it would smoke up the glass globe.

Molly, the horse, was let out for a while to gallop around. The hens were released from their house and fed some corn or yellow meal; they spent their days scratching around. There were not so many eggs in the winter and they had to be collected in a bowl.

From May until September, the situation was reversed. The cows were only brought in for milking, morning and evening, and the horse stayed out all the time, as there was plenty of grass for all of them. In the Spring some of the hens would wander off and make a nest in the briars or rushes. They were very secretive about this, and although they would sometimes turn up for feeding they would not go directly back to their nests, but would go by a circuitous route.

The first we would know about these nests was when one fine morning the hen would turn up with ten or twelve tiny yellow chicks. The ducks were the same and indeed at this time of year they seemed to almost go back to the wild. They would disappear for weeks, and then turn up with half a dozen ducklings walking in a line.

Working in the Fields

The month of March would see the start of the work in the fields. The plough was made ready and the sock would need to have a new tip put on by the blacksmith in Ballycastle. Donal Craig was a Rathlin blacksmith who had worked in America and when he returned to the island he was able to do these jobs.

Ploughing was the first task and it was heavy work. The furrows were turned over at a steady pace and the freshly turned earth came off the plough shining and reflecting the spring sunshine. Flocks of seagulls and various other birds closely followed the plough, picking up worms or other insects, of which there were plenty.

When the ploughing was completed the next task was the sowing of the crops. The newly ploughed ground would be left for a few days to dry off, then it was harrowed to break up the lumps, and if beans were to be sown they would go in first. The barley and corn followed, but as they required a finer tilth, extra harrowing was done before they were sown. After this was all done, a couple of scarecrows were put up to frighten birds away and stop them from eating the seed. The method my father used for sowing, was to tie a sheet diagonally across his shoulders, forming a sort of pouch, into which he would put a bucketful of seed. Then, walking at a steady pace up and down the field, he broadcast the seed evenly by hand.

The final stage was to harrow it in, and this would result in the seeds growing in lines a couple of inches apart. After a few weeks, if there was a drop of rain and warm weather, it would start to show above the ground in a green 'brerd', when at this stage the field was rolled with a large iron roller pulled by Molly. The next job was to prepare the ground where the potatoes were to be planted. This was usually about an acre or so, and after it had been second-ploughed to break up the ground properly, it was harrowed again and drilled with the drill plough, spaced about two feet apart.

The next task was to prepare the potato seed, which were spread out on the barn floor and the largest ones cut in two, leaving 'eyes' in both parts. This would be done a week or so before planting to give the seed a chance to dry on the cut surface. The manure was carted from the byre and stable and placed at regular intervals along the drills in small heaps or coops, after which it was 'scaled' or spread along the bottom of the drills with the four-pronged graip, and the prepared seeds were set or 'dropped' from an apron made from a sack and worn around the waist. Main crop potatoes were spaced about eighteen or twenty inches apart, and an experienced adult could work fairly fast with very little bending over. After the seeds were dropped the drills were closed with the drill plough, and that was that until the new potatoes would show above the ground in six weeks time.

From May until July daylight is almost continuous, with the sun rising about 3.30am and setting around 10.00pm. The period in between is a kind of twilight. The sun sets in the north-west and rises again in the north-east and its path can be seen just below the horizon.

Cutting Peat

Another task was cutting peat or turf in the months of May and June. We had a small peat bog on our land near the cliffs which had originally been full of water, but my father dug a deep drain out of it and at the deepest part of it was about six feet. When he finally let the water go, it went in a mighty rushing torrent, carrying dozens of eels with it over the nearby cliffs.

My father would mark out an area with the spade about twelve feet square, where he then had to skim off the top six inches or so of tough grass and roots of bog plants. This would take a day, and then the peat was ready for cutting.

The first spade's depth was brown peat with plant roots in it and after this was cut, the next layers were black peat, which was good quality. My father did the cutting and my mother would spread the cut peats close by, using a four-pronged graip.

In some parts of the bog there were six spades depth, and at the bottom there were layers of hazel nuts, some whole and some layers broken up into small bits, as if chewed by a squirrel, although squirrels do not exist on Rathlin now. After a few days, the peat was ready for moving to higher ground if the weather was dry. Here it was footed, which consisted of three peats stood on end and leaning against each other, with one put flat on top to steady them against the wind. They would then be left for a couple of weeks to dry, when the next stage was to make them into rickles. These were larger, with maybe a dozen or so peats stacked leaning on each other with plenty of air spaces for the wind to blow through.

After a month like this, they were built into a stack against a stone wall, again spaces being left for the wind. The stack would be about four or five feet high and could be any length, with the front face sloping backwards to cast off the rain. Well-dried peat is very difficult to wet, as it contains a certain amount of natural oil. When I was a bit older, I was able to help with this work, my mother would go home and bring out some tea with bread and butter and jam - this was the part which I always looked forward to.

In the winter my father carted home the dried peat with the horse and slipe as needed. It made a great fire on a winter night, very little coal was bought.

In between working at the peat cutting, there was the fieldwork to be done.

The last crop to be sown was turnips with some swedes and another large turnip called Aberdeens, which were fed to the cattle in the winter. The field was tilled very finely for these small seeds, which were sown into the tops of drills with a special seed sower pulled by Molly.

Later, when they had grown about six inches high, they had to be thinned by hand, a task which was hard work, as it required the thinner to work along the drill on his knees, which were protected by hessian sacks.

In late May my father would plant a couple of hundred cabbages, which were for the kitchen as well as for the cattle in the winter. There was little time for rest during the farming season from March until October. When the potatoes were growing well, they had to be weeded which meant going up and down the drills with a grubber pulled by the horse. This was similar to a plough, except that it had spikes or legs which rooted out the weeds. The crop was then left for a few days for the weeds to wither before the drills were moulded up again, this process being done twice during the growing season.

My father was good at building and there was a house along the road to the lighthouse, where a gable had fallen down exposing a bedroom to the elements and my father rebuilt it. He did a few hours each day when he was coming back from the lighthouse, and it is still standing seventy years later.

In the 1930s there was very little money about, so payment was made by way of barter, usually in so many days labour at the farm work when needed.

Whilst my mother helped with the potato planting and the peat cutting, as well as looking after me, she would also make the dinner which always included potatoes boiled in the three legged pot. Sometimes there would be salt fish, or fresh fish in the summer, and there was always plenty of homemade butter. Occasionally she would make champ, with a few raw eggs, scallions and butter all beaten in. There would be turnip and carrot beaten up with butter, or home-grown onions. There was always buttermilk to drink, and sometimes my father would kill a chicken or catch a rabbit and these would make great soup or stew.

Going to the Shore

We would gather limpets from the shore in the springtime and these would make tasty soup with young nettles and barley added, or anything green from the garden. Limpets are very tough to chew, so usually they would be given to the cat or dog after the soup was made, although some people would fry them in oatmeal and lard with a bit of bacon added. They could also be roasted on the open fire. Very little meat was bought and we had plenty of vegetables from our own garden, where my mother would grow carrots, leeks, beetroot, parsnips, scallions, radishes and lettuce.

We also had a garden at the shore at the base of a south-facing limestone cliff which reflected the heat of the sun on to the soil, warming it up quickly. My father would cultivate the garden early in the year, making it into rigs about four feet wide in the traditional way. He would spread a thick layer of seaweed on the rigs, then cover it with soil taken from trenches or "sheughs" at each side of the rigs. He would put seed potatoes in trays to sprout, so that around the beginning of March, they were ready for planting. This was done by digging the spade in to the soil and dropping a sprouted potato behind it. He would weed them and earth them up regularly, they were usually ready for digging at the beginning of June. They were very welcome, as by this time, the old potatoes are deteriorating in quality. He also planted Ailsa Craig onions, which thrived in the heat of the sun and were ready for pulling and drying in early August. They were then hung on ropes inside the barn rafters, a good airy place where they would keep all winter. Sometimes he would grow outdoor tomatoes, although they needed plenty of sunshine, and some years were not so good.

When I got a bit older, I would go with my mother and father to the shore garden. This was an arduous task for my small legs and it required plenty of stamina, as the garden was at the base of a two hundred and fifty feet high cliff. There was a pathway that wound its way down steep grassy slopes between the cliffs, with various hazards on the way. Briars and blackthorn were everywhere and had to be avoided and there were also ants' nests, in the form of small mounds, which I soon learned to avoid, having innocently sat on one for a rest. I soon found myself being attacked by hordes of ants of which there were two kinds – black and red – both being equally ferocious in defending their homes, and many a sting I suffered.

On these visits to the shore, we would also gather dulse if the tide was low. We would spread it out on the rounded black stones on the beach, where it would soon dry, as the stones were so hot from the June sun that you could hardly sit down on them. After a couple of hours, when the dulse was dry, we would gather it up and it made a sound like rustling paper as it was packed into a hessian sack. My father carried the sack on his back, while my mother would carry a small bag of new potatoes, as well as carrying or pulling me back up the cliff path.

While at the shore, my father would make a fire from driftwood and boil up a saucepan for a cup of tea, sometimes putting a couple of eggs in the pan to boil at the same time. We would also have some soda bread with butter.

There was a small stream, which tumbled over the cliff just a few yards from the garden and it was very handy for watering the plants. Sometimes a local fishing boat would pass by, and they would stop and exchange fresh fish for new potatoes.

I loved paddling in the sea and then stepping on the black stones, which were warmed by the sun. There was very little sand. The stones in the sea were very slippery as they were covered in all sorts of seaweed, and many a time I fell in and had to be rescued by my mother.

By the time we got home I was tired out and ready for a sleep. My father would milk the cows, while my mother made the dinner, which would be new potatoes and fresh fish. These idyllic days have remained in my memory.

The dulse was stored until there was enough to fill a large sack tightly packed, which my father would then take to Ballycastle, and send it by rail to a shop called Bradley's in Belfast. There was always a demand for it in the city.

Kelp Making

Another shore based industry was kelp making, although in the 1930s it was declining. My father didn't bother with it, there was a kelp kiln close to the shore garden.

The large broad leaf kelp and tangles were gathered and dried above high tide mark by hanging over rock outcrops or low stone walls built for the purpose. In the month of May there was often a westerly gale. The rough seas would loosen large amounts of the previous year's kelp crop and pile it up on the shore. This was known as the May Fleece. Old people used to say that there would be no summer, if there was no May Fleece.

After it was gathered and dried, the next job was to burn it in a kiln, set in the ground and constructed of beach stones, being about six feet long by two and a half feet wide and two feet deep. A fire was started with heather, whins and driftwood, and when it was going properly, it was time to start feeding the rods into it. This process could continue for a night and a day, until all the kelp was burned. It would gradually become a molten mass, which had to be stirred or "run" with iron kelp rods. When all was complete, the kiln was left for a couple of days to cool down and the kelp had hardened like rock. It was then broken up with a heavy hammer and cold chisel.

In earlier times, the landlord would arrange for it to be shipped out and sold in Scotland, the sale price being set against rents owed. But, as the landlord no longer controlled the island in the 1930s, other arrangements were made for its sale. A puffer (small steamboat) came in from Carnlough, tying up at the end of the Sheep House Pier. The kelp was loaded on to it and the islanders had to take whatever price they were offered. I remember hearing my father and Mickey Joe talking about it, and they said that the islanders were robbed, so by the 1940s, this ancient industry closed forever.

Kelp was used in a number of industries, the main extracts were potash and iodine. This latter was used as an antiseptic, and of course potash was used as a fertiliser in farming, and also for soap making. It is still used in a number of industries, although it is no longer burnt, there are more modern ways of extracting the chemicals from it. An old record states that twenty tons of seaweed made one ton of kelp from which eight pounds of iodine was extracted. By the 1930s the price had fallen to £2 per ton, so it was no longer worth all of the hard work involved.

The Arrival of the Birds

March and April would see the arrival of various sea and land birds, the black-headed gull being among the first. It is a very noisy bird, always arguing and quarrelling over nest sites, which are built in freshwater loughs where there are reeds or rushes. The snipe would start making their eerie sounds after dark, which was caused by diving at speed through the air with the wind whistling through the wing feathers. When I was small this sound frightened me as there were stories that the sounds were made by ghosts or lost souls.

The skylark would arrive as well as the lapwing or peewit, and in May came the cuckoo, followed later by the corncrake which would keep us awake at night. Many thousands of seabirds - puffins, guillemots and others, would take up residence on the cliffs at the west lighthouse in May, where they raised their young, then departing in July to spend the rest of the year on the ocean.

There was a good deal of rock climbing for birds eggs, and some families specialised in it. Probably the high point for this activity, was in the early years of the Second World War.

Food rationing led to people resorting to trapping rabbits or gathering wild birds eggs, the latter commanding good prices in Belfast. The eggs were incorporated in dried egg powder, which was a substitute for real eggs. In this form it wasn't possible to tell their origin. One young man, Joe McCurdy, a cousin of mine, was killed in a cliff fall, climbing for eggs.

The best known of Rathlin's climbers was Paddy "the climber" Morrison, who lived before my time. I have only seen photos of him, apart from the numerous stories of his exploits.

He was a big man and completely fearless, and of the many stories of him, I will mention a couple here. If Paddy was of a mind to go climbing, and couldn't find anyone to go with him to help with the ropes, he would take his horse. When they got to the cliffs, Paddy would drive a crowbar into the ground, to which he fastened the hand rope. He then tied the body rope to the hind leg of his horse, which stood quietly eating grain from a nosebag. Paddy would then go over the edge and down the cliff, returning half an hour later with a good bag of eggs, and perhaps also a bird or two. The horse was still standing in the same place chewing away as if it was an everyday task. It was said that he placed great reliance on the horse obeying any command. If he got into difficulty, he could call to the horse, which would immediately walk away from the cliff, pulling him back up again with the body rope.

Paddy was one of the island's great characters. He did not see eye to eye with the landlord, and many a difference of opinion they had according to the stories. Paddy usually came off best in these encounters.

Another story told of him, concerned planks of wood which came ashore from a sunken ship, in a place which was only accessible by boat. Now the landlord, Mr Gage, claimed the right to all timber which was washed ashore, so he organised his own boat and crew to go and collect the planks.

Paddy Morrison knew that the timber was there, so off he set with his horse and ropes to collect it before the landlord's boat got there. It did not take him long to get the planks hauled up the cliffs, and carted back to his house, the horse being a faithful and willing accomplice.

The landlord was enraged when his boat crew returned without the timber, so he started making enquiries. One of his spies told him where the timber was, so he sent for Paddy to come and see him. Paddy duly went, and the landlord told him that he would have to bring the timber to him. Paddy protested that he had found the timber first, but he was told that he had no choice in the matter, the landlord said to him "I have the authority".

Paddy delivered the planks to Mr Gage, and that was the end of the matter, until an occasion later in the year, when Mr Gage was in the upper end with visitors, shooting rabbits and ducks. They chanced to cross Paddy's farm. He was out working in the field and ignored them. However Paddy had a cross bull, who took exception to the landlord's shooting party and chased them. Mr Gage shouted to Paddy for help, but Paddy called back "Show him your papers of authority, the same as you did to me" and continued working. Well the landlord and his guests managed to scramble over a stone wall before the bull caught them, their dignity was in tatters, as Paddy's neighbours, on hearing the shouting, had come out just in time to see the landlord and his party being pursued by the bull.

While my father was doing all of his farm work, he also had part-time employment as attendant at the West Lighthouse where he would do relief duty for any lighthouse keeper who was on leave or ill. These duties, which were in four-hour shifts, were often at weekends. Sometimes keepers would take a day or two off to be with their families at the East Lighthouse, where each keeper was allocated a house, so my father would do a Saturday night and Sunday. I can remember walking with my mother, or being pushed in a buggy, the two miles to the lighthouse over rough roads on a Sunday. We would have tea at the lighthouse and then walk back with my father if his duty spell had ended, but this was not always so, as some keepers would not arrive back until midnight.

Fishing

My father would go fishing from the rocks when the tides were right during August and September.

Rock fishing was carried out with a bamboo rod ten or twelve feet long, which had been bought in Ballycastle in Sharpe and McKinley's hardware shop.

There were various fishing rocks, one of which was Doon, a large rock stack near the West Lighthouse which was a good place for catching lythe (pollack) and morans. The lythe were very popular on the island, some of them being eight or nine pounds in weight when caught off the Rock and even larger when caught from a boat. Morans, also known as wrasse, were a very bony fish and not so popular.

My father fishing on Doon rock at Bull Point.
The saucepan was for boiling limpets as bait.

Other fishing rocks are Sron Deargan and Sron Liath, which were good for lythe. There are good rocks on the north side of the island, but they are hard to access, and can be dangerous when there are big ocean swells. Killeany pier was popular with the upper end men for fishing, after the quarry closed in 1927, but it gradually disintegrated until it was no longer safe. I can remember being there on a Sunday evening, when there were a dozen men from Brockley, Ballygill and Cleggan, fishing for Glashan and Lythe. There was plenty of space for everybody, as the pier deck was large.

The fishing line used was a heavy hemp cord, with the last couple of yards made from what was called catgut, or else from horsehair taken from the horse's tail, and twisted into a fine line.

The bait would often be a small white feather or a small strip of fish, or a rubber eel for lythe and boiled limpets were also used. I can recall my father using an old saucepan in which he would boil the limpets for bait. He would grind them up in a hollow in the rock, and then throw handfuls out to attract the fish, this was called "frassing" from the Gaelic meaning 'plenty'. Alternatively, if there was no means of boiling them, he would grind limpets in their shells in a hollow in the rock, and throw them out. Around the island these holes can be seen at good fishing rocks, where they have been made over centuries of grinding up limpets in the same spot.

The larger fish would be split, salted and hung out to dry in the sun and wind. When dry, they were hung inside from the rafters and made a good dinner on a winter's day.

Other fish caught from a boat were 'glashans', also very popular. They could be up to twenty pounds or more in weight and they were also salted and dried for the winter. Mackerel were common during the summer months as they swam in large shoals and were caught from a boat with a hand line. They were very nice when cooked on the day of catching, together with new potatoes and buttermilk, however, it was difficult to cure them as they are a very oily fish.

Several families on the island fished full time and their boats were all of a similar size being about twenty feet long and clinker built from larch or pine.

There are various boat builders along the coast from Donegal to Antrim, the oldest of these is McDonalds, of Moville in Donegal, who have been building boats since 1750.

These boats are known as Drontheims, a name which is derived from the port in Norway called Trondheim, where they were first built and exported to the Irish coast.

The method of fishing was by long line, which would be anything from a hundred yards up to a quarter of a mile in length, with hooks every couple of yards. It would be baited up in the evening with pieces of fish, then coiled neatly in the boat and was set around dusk. To keep it near the surface, it would have large corks spaced out every few feet, with round metal or glass marker floats spaced every twenty or so yards.

This line was lifted again at dawn, which in the summertime was around three a.m. This had to be done, because if it was left until full daylight, seals would attack and destroy any fish on the line.

The catch was mainly conger eel, skate and dogfish, which were sold to the fish merchant in Ballycastle. The latter are a form of small shark, and have a very rough skin like sandpaper. Skinned before being sold, they would later appear in fishmongers' shops in the city under the name of 'rock cod'. There were also plenty of lobsters and crabs caught, although there was little demand for crab.

In the late autumn another form of fishing was the hauling of shore-based nets. Several families would have a share in a net, and upwards of twenty men could be involved in a haul. which was carried out before the start of the ebb-tide.   When the ebb starts to run, the fish go out into deeper water and stay there until the flood starts. The best time for fishing off the rocks or net hauling is when it is just getting dusk, and it would be dark by the time the haul was over,

One net rope would be secured by a team on shore, and then a boat would take the net out a few hundred yards and gradually set it in a semi-circle, the other end rope being brought ashore further along where another team would take it. The boat would stay on the outside of the net in case it snagged on the sea bed, when the men could free it with a boat hook.

Both teams would then start to haul the net ashore, getting soaking wet in the process. During this operation, it was important to keep an even pull at both ends. The boat crew would keep watch and if one team was pulling stronger than the other, they would call in Gaelic, Tarrain Thiar (pull west) or Tarrain Thoir (pull east).

There would be a variety of fish in the net and once it was ashore, the catch was divided out in shares and there would be a share for the boat as well as its crew. Once the fish had been divided into piles on the shore, one person, usually a young one, would be asked to turn their back, while one man would call out "whose share is this?", pointing to one pile of fish. The person whose back was turned would call out a name. In this way all the piles of fish were allocated, and no-one would argue about the size of their share, as all agreed that this was a fair way of doing it.

There were a number of good fishing marks around the island and various landmarks were in use to locate them. Killeany bank was one of these and the landmarks were - row out from Killeany shore until you can see the chimney of John McPhee's house. If you also have the chimneys of the Post Office and the other station houses in line you are on the fishing ground. This was always a good place for catching mackerel. Other fishing marks were Tollavey Bank near Bull Point, the high bank in Church Bay, and the wreck of the *Drake*.

North of Cantruan Head was a good place for very large glashan (coalfish). There were other marks off the east side of the island, which was once a good place for hake in an easterly gale.

West of Bull Point, right out to the undersea reef known as Shamrock Pinnacle, was probably the best fishing mark. As well as island boats, there were always boats from Ballintoy and Dunseverick, who had a long row and sail, but the catches made it worthwhile. One fish caught here in large quantities was ling, which when dried and salted were very popular with farmers from the mainland. Mackerel would arrive in shoals following the herring fry, and we would always know when they were about, as large numbers of seagulls would gather in flocks, catching the herring fry. The mackerel would take any bait, a jig was used for catching them, a wooden frame holding up to a dozen baited hooks, attached to a heavy hemp line. When it was dropped over the side of a boat, the mackerel would swarm to it, and so within a few minutes, you might have a dozen fish on the jig. I can remember us filling a couple of fish boxes in half an hour.

Tides, Weather, Storms and Boats

As we depended on boats to get to the mainland, tides and weather played an important part in our lives.

One of the main hazards, is the ebb tide, which is an immense body of water which flows out of the Irish Sea twice a day. Running past Rathlin on both sides like a mighty river, it returns as the flood tide, and is compressed into a fairly narrow channel between Rue na Faoileann (Point of the Seagulls) on Rathlin and Fair Head on the mainland. The west-going ebb picks up speed, and if there should be a strong or gale force wind coming from the north west direction it gets up to a ferocious sea. The churning water makes a roaring sound like a waterfall, as neither the wind nor tide will give way.

These tides are caused by the gravity of the moon's pull. Twice a month there are spring tides, which occur at new moon and full moon, when the sun and moon are pulling in the same direction. In between these are what are known as neep tides.

There are two main bodies, or bushes, in the ebb as it flows through the channel, and boats coming from or going to Ballycastle will make for the gap between the bushes. This is relatively calm, and if you miss this you will have to wait until the main force of the tide has gone and then go around the back of it. A good knowledge of the tides and their times is essential, as they are later each day by about fifty minutes.

Of course, if you know the tides well, they can be a help. Leaving Rathlin or Ballycastle at the right time, the tide will be with you for a good part of the journey, lifting you along. I remember an old man telling me that it sometimes took as long as five hours in a sailing boat to make the journey to Rathlin if the tide was against you. Coming out of Ballycastle he would run westward as far as Sheep Island, then he would tack across to Bull Point and then back along the shore to O'Berne.

The Gheogan is a tide that runs westwards close to the shore near Bull Point, while the Clachan is another tide running west of Bull Point. These tides were very useful when fishing in a sailing or rowing boat.

Sometimes in the winter, westerly gales would blow up and there would be no boats operating for maybe a week. The longest period I know of without a boat, occurred in February 1938, when nothing crossed the channel for 24 days. Supplies in the shops ran very low, so a small plane was sent in with some basic foodstuffs, although those who lived on farms had their own milk, butter, eggs, home baked bread, potatoes, vegetables and dried fish, which they shared with those who had no land. Things were not as bad as the newspapers made out.

People knew how to read the natural weather signs, as there were no weather forecasts in those days. Here are some of the sayings I remember, and they were generally reliable.

A red sky at night, good weather next day.
A red sky in the morning, windy and wet weather ahead.
Goat's hair or mare's tail cloud foretells stormy weather soon.
Very high sheep's wool cloud, good weather ahead.
Tall clouds like mountains meant thunder.
A ring around the moon, rain next day.
Mock sun also forecast rain.
Green patches in the sky meant more rain.
Cattle standing on top of a hill, good weather.
Heavy swell on the sea breaking high over Carrick Manannan
  rock meant storm coming.
Waves cracking sharply on the shore, east wind next day.
Low black cloud, rain is close.
Pet day or very nice day follows bad weather means more bad
weather.
Geese flying south, high and fast, winter weather coming.
Geese flying north, spring is on the way.
Birds flying low, rain and wind ahead.
Rain before seven, clear before eleven.
Rain after eleven, rain all day.

This weather lore guided people in both boating and farming.

The Neighbours

Our nearest neighbours were the Blacks of Glacklugh. Mrs Teresa Black lived there with her son Paddy and daughter Tessie, her husband having died in 1919. Her other sons Michael, James, Kevin and John worked away from the island. Their farm was the same size as ours. Like most older women, Mrs Black was always dressed in black, wearing a long dress or skirt down to the ground, and a black blouse, and if going out, a black shawl thrown over their head and shoulders

Paddy was a very good singer, as were his brothers John, Kevin and James and they were also good musicians who could play a range of instruments.

Our other close neighbours were the Andersons of Glackanacre. Mickey Joe lived there with his wife Mary, but they did not have a family. He was a second cousin of my father and was a very tall man. His wife was often in poor health, although some people thought that it was 'put on.' His nephew, Seamus McCurdy, worked full time with him. Mickey Joe was always doing something interesting. He built a forge by quarrying a space out of the hill beside the house, and then putting a roof on it, he made shoes for his horses, as well as other ironwork. I would often visit him and stand by the fire watching him hammering the red-hot iron into horseshoes on the anvil. He also developed a method of building using a timber frame, over which chicken wire and hessian were tightly stretched. This was then plastered with several coats of cement and sand.

Mickey Joe was very good with horses, and he would talk to them, calming them down. When I was about eleven or twelve years old I could ride a young horse bareback, without saddle, halter or reins. I sometimes got the job of being the first on the back of a young horse helping to break it in. Mickey Joe would first walk the horse around the field, holding it by the forelock with me on its back. When the horse got used to me being on its back, he would let it go, it would set off at a fast trot across the field, with me holding on to its mane and forelock.

Sometimes a nervous horse would try to get rid of me by rising up on its hind legs. I soon found that the best way to deal with this, was to pull hard on its forelock. This would bring its head up, and it was now in danger of going over backwards, so it would soon drop its front feet to the ground, I always had a lot of strength in my arms. I would also talk quietly to them, this calmed them, and the half gallop would slow to a trot and finally to a standstill back where Mickey Joe was standing. We knew then, that the young horse was well on the way to doing his share of farmwork.

Mickey Joe always had a lot of stories of events which had happened in the past, including ghost stories.

The author on horseback c.1940

My paternal grandmother, Catherine, was an aunt of Mickey Joe, and my father was also related to the Blacks, whose farms were also about fifty acres, which was the average on the island. It was at this time that the Land Act was brought in by the Government, which allowed all the tenant farmers to buy their freehold from the landlord, thus ending the system, which had existed for nearly two hundred years.

In the old port of Oweyberne c.1900
l.to r. Paddy Morrison (the climber), John Michael McCurdy
(Cleggan) in foreground with beard and hat. John Phairic McCurdy
far right with hat. The others are visitors. The boats are the
traditional Dronthiems.

The three families worked together in a number of ways, one of which was in the matter of boats.

Over a period of several generations they jointly owned a number of boats which were always known as the Garvagh boat. They were used to bring in supplies such as turf from Ballycastle, boating out cattle and fishing. Although the main harbour was often used for landing supplies, the boats were kept in an old fishing port called O'Berne which was closer to the houses and also the fishing grounds. This was important in the days before boats had engines. The port was on land shared by our family and the Blacks and it was common grazing of about twenty acres, known as Pairc Mor. Adjoining it was Pairc Beag, of about five acres, which was owned by the Andersons.

This port was also shared with a couple of other boats known as the Cleggan boats, although access to it from the land, was more difficult for them. For a time the Brockley boat used the west port in O'Berne, although they transferred to Killeany after the limestone quarry there was closed.

The Garvagh boat owners had constructed a slide road right down into the port. This allowed them to take a horse and slide almost to the boat, and load on any heavy items such as bags of meal or coal. Even cattle were brought into this port at times and driven up the pathway from the shore to the cliff top. The slide was constructed like a large sledge with iron shod runners which would slide easily over grass or heather, and it could be used in places where a cart could not be taken.

As I got a bit older, I would often go to O'Berne, as there was always someone there working on boats: painting, tarring, repairing the hull or even installing an engine. There were lobster creels to be repaired in the winter, and after a storm the slipway had to be cleared of big stones rolled along by the sea. It was always my favourite place.

There were three caves, which were used for storing everything - timber, ropes, lobster creels and cans of tar, one of the caves also had a boat in it.

I was getting to know who people were in our part of the island. There were six other households of McCurdys, although only two of these were related to us, both through the Anderson connection.

Five of the McCurdy families were known by a patronym ie. derived from an ancestor. I must have been eight or nine years old before I realised that they were all McCurdys.

*An early Garvagh boat unloading peat brought from Ballycastle, L.
to R. My grandfather Joseph McCurdy, standing by mast with hat,
John Black, Glacklugh, just behind mast with hat.
Mickey Joe Anderson with peaked cap, His father Joseph "Michael
Jack" Anderson, note horse standing quietly in water. c. 1900*

*L to R. Mickey Joe Anderson and his wife Mary
Bridget and Joseph (Michael Jack) Mickey Joe's parents.
Front L to R. Jack Scott (Light Keeper) his sister Tessie Scott, small
boy behind Tessie is Joe McCurdy, next is his sister Bridget, they
were grandchildren of Bridget and Joseph, seated are Clare and Mary
Anderson who kept the post office.*

l.to r.: Seamus McCurdy,
Mickey Joe Anderson and
myself seated in a cart with a
lamb and its mother

Killeany Limestone Quarry
l.to r.: John "Roe" McCurdy, South Cleggan, John"Beag" McCurdy,
South Cleggan, Michael Craig, Ballygill North, John Kelly Cuil na g
Cnoc. c. 1900

*My cousin Lily McNearney with myself in buggy,
looking like I need a haircut.*

*McPhee family, The Bridge,
Rathlin, 1922
L to R. Jeannie, John (senior),
unknown, Mary, Nora,
John (junior)*

Courtesy Ian McLean.

There was Daniel 'John Ban' McCurdy and his wife Rose, nee McAuley who was from Glenshesk near Ballycastle. He was a farmer and was also a good rock climber and they lived in Kinraver townland but they had no family.

Patrick 'Michael' McCurdy was a farmer and a good blacksmith who lived with his widowed sister Mary in Lower Cleggan.

John 'Michael' McCurdy and his wife Mary Ann lived in Upper Cleggan with John's mother Catriona. Alex Morrison also lived there as Catriona was his great aunt. Alex was brought from Greenock in Scotland to live with them at the age of four, when his mother died from influenza in 1919. Daniel, Patrick and John were brothers.

A different branch of the McCurdys was John 'Pharaic' McCurdy who also lived in Upper Cleggan with his two sisters, Lizzie, and widowed sister Peggy Murphy along with her son Owen who was known as 'Ownie'. Mrs Murphy's husband had died in Liverpool and she returned to live in Rathlin.

There was also Johnnie Black and his sister Annie who lived in North Kinraver. There were no children in any of these households and as they were also many years older than my parents, they seemed to me to be extremely old and remote.

All of the old women wore long black skirts, down to the ground, as well as a black blouse and a black shawl around their head and shoulders. As a youngster I was a bit afraid of them, as none of them had children and they were not very tolerant of the young generation.

There had also been another McCurdy family, known as the 'John Roes', but they had left the island to live on a farm near Ballycastle before I was born.

There were the Brockley McCurdys, related to us on the Anderson side but as they lived well off the main road, we did not have much contact with them.

The Upper Cleggan and Kinraver McCurdys as well as Daniel McFaul, Annie Black and Frank Craig were all fluent Irish speakers.

James McCurdy lived in Lower Cleggan with his wife Catherine (Cassie) who was a first cousin of my father through the Anderson side. They were known as the "John Beags". There were three boys, Sean, Seamus, and Joey, who were a good few years older than me, and Michael, who was the same age. There had been another brother Patsy, who died young, and then there were three girls who were a few years older than me. Bridget was the oldest, the younger two, Mary and Lily, would often visit our house and take me out for a run in my buggy.

Their father James was a good accordion player and I can remember the occasional Sunday afternoon in the summer when he would bring his accordion to a hill called Droim along the road near their house. There he would sit and play and was sometimes joined by one or two others. My father played the fiddle, and would sit out on a wall at our house playing and if any of the Black family were about they would also join in with the pipes or fiddle, thus music could be heard all over our part of the island on a summer Sunday.

The McCurdy girls Lily and Mary were very good singers, as were their brothers Seamus and Joey and Seamus was also a good accordion player.

The three sisters.
l. to r. Lily, Mary and Bridget McCurdy.
Courtesy Gabrielle McCurdy

James and his brother John ran a boat known as the Lighthouse Boat, as they had a contract with the Commissioners of Irish Lights to bring lighthouse keepers and supplies to the island. Their boat went from the island every Tuesday and as it was the only regular Rathlin boat, islanders who needed any supplies from Ballycastle would go and return with it. They had a third crew member known as John Joe McCurdy, who lived at "the station" and he was noted for being very cantankerous as he would not give a civil answer to anyone.

The only other boat which ran on a regular basis was owned by Johnny Coyle of Ballycastle, who had a contract with the Post Office to bring the mail to and from Rathlin on Monday, Wednesday and Friday. He would bring supplies for the two shops and the island pub, and the Ballycastle bakers would send a tea chest packed with fresh baked bread, although many families would not buy "shop bread".

Johnny also brought visitors in the summer who would walk to the West Lighthouse to see the seabirds, a distance of about five miles each way. As youngsters we called these people hikers. In those times the lighthouse was manned, so visitors were not allowed to go down the steps to it, however, a good view of the birds could be had from the cliff top.

Daniel McFaul and his wife Mary Ann had a farm about a mile or so further along the main road from us, called Glack an Toighe Mor, "the big house in the hollow", in the townland of Kinramer South. They had four sons, Daniel, Neal, James and John, and two daughters Lily and Rosie and, in addition to farming, they worked at fishing and kept their boat in the old port of Cooraghy.

Cornelius Maguire and his wife Margaret lived in Brockley, in the townland of Ballygill Middle with their family, Mary, Kate, Neilly, Seamus, Frank and the youngest Philomena, who used to call for me to take me to school when I first started.

Other families in Brockley were Frank Craig, who lived with his sister Annie, and John and Dan McCurdy who lived with their sister Kate. These McCurdys were related to us through the

Anderson connection as their mother Margaret, was a sister of my grandmother Catherine. Sometimes I would visit them and I always remember Kate spinning wool on her spinning wheel. There were four families by the name of Black who, as far as I know, were not related to each other. Johnnie Black lived in North Kinraver with his sister Annie. A brother of theirs, Alan, had been drowned in a boating accident before I was born. I do not remember Johnnie as he died when I was young, although, from stories I heard, he was a very argumentative man, and would challenge others to a fight. He challenged an uncle of mine, Michael McNearney from Belfast, but he picked on the wrong man as he was left with a bloody nose. I was afraid of his sister Annie, always being dressed in black, she was very stern and I thought that she was a witch. I remember hearing a story told, that Johnnie Black had a dressing gown sent to him by a relative in America and never having seen one before, he wore it one Sunday to Church, thinking that it was an American style of coat.

There was Loughie Black and Robert who lived with their widowed mother Mary Jane in Ballygill. Robert got married and went to live in Belfast where another brother, Paddy, lived with his daughter Mairead. This family was always known by the nickname "Red" as they had red hair. Loughie and Robert were very strong men and Loughie was always ready to fight. I heard a story told of Robert when he went to work in Glasgow. He was walking back to his digs on a Friday night with his pay packet in his pocket. He was set upon by two villains who tried to take his money, but Robert using all his strength, grabbed hold of the two heroes and rammed their heads into a wall. He then walked on, leaving them lying unconscious on the street.

The other family of Blacks, who also lived in Ballygill, were Patrick and his wife Susan, and to distinguish them from the other Blacks they were known as the Paddy Uilleams, (William) after an ancestor.

The brothers Daniel and Sandy Maguire lived in Knockans townland and they were related to the Maguires of Brockley.

There was a family of Andersons living in Shandragh, but they left the island and went to live in Dublin when I was young. James Hegarty lived alone in Shandragh while other members of his family lived in the harbour area or "Station" which was called after the old coastguard station.

There was a Scottish family, McLean, who lived at the "Bridge" in Knockans. The house took its name from a stone built bridge over a stream, which ran under the main road. Their grandfather, John Mc Phee, had come to Rathlin as quarry master at Killeany limestone quarry, which was operated by a Mr Johnston.

Boat trip around Rathlin c.1922.
Man at stern (with cap) is Johnny Coyle, Ballycastle
boat owner. To his right is Pat Johnston (aged 7). To her
right is her mother Mrs Johnston, Killeany quarry
owners. In front of J. Coyle is John McPhee (with hat)
quarry master and to his left is Mrs McPhee

Courtesy of Ian McLean

My First visit to Belfast

My first cousins in Belfast, Patsy and Lily McNearney, who were nieces of my mother, were a few years older than me, and most years they would come to Rathlin for a few weeks in the summer.

l. to r.: Patsy McNearney holding my brother Ronnie.
Lily, with myself standing in front.
I think that the trousers were made by my mother.

Ronnie was born in June 1935, and as my father was busy and my Rathlin grandparents were both dead, I was bundled off to my other grandparents in the city.

My uncle Hugh and his two nieces, Patsy and Lily, collected me in Ballycastle, where my father had taken me on the boat. This was the biggest adventure of my life, as we set off on the narrow gauge train for Ballymoney. I had never seen a train before and I can remember the hard wooden slatted seats in the carriage, and the trees and houses flashing past the window.

When we arrived in Ballymoney, we had to wait for the main line train from Derry to Belfast, which came rushing into the station, all clouds of smoke, steam and noise.

This was a more comfortable train, which stopped at larger towns such as Ballymena and Antrim but whizzed through other small stations.

Arriving into York Street station in Belfast, the next big surprise was boarding a tram to get to my Granny's house. I had never seen so many people before. As we travelled on the tram along the Crumlin road, my uncle pointed out places to me such as the Mater Hospital, and then the prison. After that was Ewart's flax spinning mill, and standing out on the hill was Holy Cross Church, with its twin spires.

I soon got used to the noise on the streets, with lots of people walking past the house, and horses and carts delivering coal, bread, and milk. Men with handcarts came around selling fish on Fridays. The street lamps were a novelty to me as they worked on gas and were lit by a man who would come around the streets in the evening.

The children would fix a rope to the top crosspiece of the lamp post and use it as a swing. I soon learned some of the street games. There was marbles played on the pavement, hopscotch and skipping played by the girls, football played by the boys, and another game played by girls was the spinning top using a whip to keep it spinning. The only time when we children went into the house, was to get something to eat which was usually a 'piece', of bread and jam. Soon it was teatime, and after that, out for another hour or two before bedtime.

I stayed with my granny for about two months and got to know all my other cousins. There was Dominic, Gerard, and Michael, who were older than me, and Roy and Rita who were younger than me. Some years later, they all emigrated to the United States, as their father, my uncle Michael, was an American citizen who was born when my grandparents lived there in the 1880/1890s.

I also got to know the other children in the street who would come to the door and ask if I could go out to play. I think that I was looked on as some kind of a novelty, coming from an island in the ocean, of which they had no experience.

I liked the city and was, in a way, sorry to leave it. Little did I know then, that I would be coming back to live in it sooner than I thought, but I had to go back to Rathlin. My uncle brought me back to Ballycastle on the train, where my father was waiting to bring me home on the boat and the reality finally dawned on me that I had a new brother. No longer was I the main centre of attention.

Visits to Ballycastle

My father would go to Ballycastle from time to time, usually to one of the fairs, which were held on the third Tuesday of the month. There was the May fair held on the last Tuesday of the month, and it was also known as the Spring hiring fair, where farmers would hire boys for six months for £5 plus keep. Generally they were treated as slaves, having to work six days a week from early morning until late evening. If we misbehaved ourselves, we were threatened with being sent to the hiring fair.

My father would buy a few score of cabbage plants for planting out in the field, and they were used for feeding cattle in the winter, as well as for the table (a score is twenty). The gooseberry fair was held on the last Tuesday of July, and as its name indicates, there was large quantities of soft fruit, including gooseberries for sale.

The largest fair was the Lammas which was held on the last Monday and Tuesday of August and when I got older I was allowed to go to it with my father. There were amusements of every sort, such as dodgem cars, chair-a-planes and swing boats which fascinated me. There were stalls galore selling every imaginable thing such as dulse and yellow man and every sort of sweets, which attracted hordes of wasps from everywhere. I used to think, that just like people, they knew the time of the fair, and would come from as far away as Tyrone, setting off a week before to get there on time. Everything that would be needed on a farm was for sale - ropes, tools and harness for the horses.

My father would buy a coil of rope which he used for reins for the horse as well as other jobs, he would also buy a few balls of coir rope for tying down thatch or corn stacks, or sometimes a new scythe blade, or a new zinc or enamel bucket. For me the highlight of the fair, was getting a new pair of leather boots for going to school in the winter. These were known as sparbled boots, the soles of which were protected by rows of small metal studs. There was also a heavier sort called hob-nailed boots, which were worn by men for work and the studs on these soles were larger and heavier. If I was lucky I would also get a pair of Wellingtons or rubber boots, which I really liked and I would test them out in puddles or small loughs of water. If the water came in over the top I then got a telling off.

Large numbers of cattle, horses, ponies and donkeys were for sale, as this was the main fair for buying and selling livestock. We would meet lots of people my father knew, some who were from Rathlin who had gone to live on the mainland, such as the John Roe McCurdys from Cleggan, who lived at Carn Dhu outside Ballycastle. My father had gone to school with them, and they would go into a pub for a couple of half-uns and talk of farming and old times. This was the point when I would be given a few shillings to spend on whatever I wanted, and given strict instructions to meet my father at the pier to catch the boat home. The first thing which I would buy was a new penknife - I had been eyeing them up on the stalls earlier, then a bag of assorted sweets, before heading off the amusements on the seafront. Some of the young men and bigger boys would stay overnight, and there were usually dances held in the Antrim Arms and the Royal Hotel which they would go to, coming home the next morning on whatever fishing boats were over from the island, or cadging a lift back on an Islay boat on its way home.

The Islay people were always at the fair, they would come in their boats to sell salt fish, which were in great demand by all the people from the country areas. The Islay people mostly spoke Gaelic and they always got on well with the Rathlin people whose Gaelic was close to their dialect.

Starting School

I was about to enter a totally new world at the end of the summer. Another phase of my life was about to begin, as it was time for me to start school. Up until now I had run around as wild and free as a rabbit, but those days were now at an end.

I was not impressed with the thought of being confined to a classroom all day. I think that I was influenced by hearing older children saying that they did not like school. Anyhow there was no getting out of it. In the words of an old woman who lived near us, "what can't be cured must be endured".

It was a walk of over two miles to school with a few steep hills on the way. My father took me there in the mornings, and in the afternoon my mother would meet me.

After a while I got quite independent and preferred to walk home with the rest of the scholars. There were eight others going to our part of the island, most of whom were older than me, so if there was any sort of strife, I relied on my three cousins for support.

As I got used to school, I began to enjoy it. There were forty-five pupils ranging in age from myself up to fourteen in seven standards or classes. The majority were from the lower end of the island, but as I only saw them at school, I didn't know them so well.

We had two teachers, Mrs Sally Black the Principal, who took the older children, and assistant teacher, Miss O'Boyle taught the younger ones, including teaching us some Irish.

At lunchtime we would quickly eat whatever we had brought with us, usually a few slices of barley or soda bread with butter and a bottle of milk to drink. If we were thirsty, we would get a drink of water from a well alongside the road which was called the Pound Well. It was named after a small field next to it which was once used by the landlord as a pound for stray cattle. We would lie down and scoop water up in our hands. Passing horses would also drink from it.

*The principal teacher, Mrs Sally Black nee McPolin,
with class, c. 1940s*

There was no playground at the school, so the boys played football in a field nearby which belonged to the parish and often had cows grazing in it. The goalposts would be a couple of jerseys at each end. The surface, which was short grass with some thistles growing, had another hazard that was to be avoided - pats of cow manure which, in the heat of a match, were not always possible to avoid. Sometimes we would slip or get pushed into it, which would start a row. There was rarely a referee, so the bigger boys dictated the rules. We had little understanding, or cared even less for such refinements as the off-side rule. A goal was a goal, whether by fair means or foul. As the field sloped from one end to the other, the team at the top end had the advantage.

At other times we would play a game which had two teams, one called Hounds and the other one the Hares. The hares would run off first as fast as they could to find somewhere to hide from the pursuing hounds who would take up the chase after about five minutes. As no one had a watch, it was always guesswork. If the hares could get back to school without being caught, they were the winners.

There were times when the lack of a timepiece worked against us as we would get back to school late, and then the piper had to be paid. There was always a supply of sally rods for use as canes and if one broke, somebody was sent to cut another one from the bushes across the road. Sometimes the braver ones would put a nick in the cane with a penknife, and so it would soon break. Heaven help the culprit if he or she was found out.

The girls played their own games, hide and seek being one, or else a game with a ball, such as rounders.

One thing we were not short of was exercise, with all these games and then walking home.

Some of the children were from the East Lighthouse where they lived in houses built there for families of Irish Lighthouse Keepers and I can remember being invited to parties there.

In the springtime when we were going to school there was always lots going on in the fields, as all the farmers would be out in March and April ploughing and getting ready for sowing and planting. As they ploughed they were followed by flocks of seagulls and other birds who snatched every worm which was turned up in the furrow.

Coming Home from School

At three o'clock lessons ended so we were free to go home, and in good weather we would go by various routes, anywhere but the main road, it would sometimes take us a couple of hours to get home.

There was a rabbit warren along the road at the top of a hill called Doige and as soon as we appeared, scores of rabbits would dash down the holes. We would try to reach them, but without much success as rabbits always have at least one escape hole, and there were a lot of whins (gorse) in our way.

In the springtime, black headed gulls nested in a couple of marshy loughs in a hilly area near the road. They built their nests on tufts of grass or rushes, or small islands in the water. We would take off our boots and wade out to the nests, sometimes slipping and falling in but we did not rob the nests. We just wanted to see if there were any eggs in them and also to see what the gulls would do.

The gulls were ferocious in defence of their nests. They would dive bomb us, coming within inches of our heads and screaming loudly at us, and they always managed to drive us off.

We were always on the look out for other birds' nests, such as lapwings, or peewits as we called them, which nested in tufts of heather in damp areas. If we got close to them, the adult bird would lead us away from the nest, by flying a short distance and pretending to be injured and if we ran towards it then it would fly off again and repeat the ruse.

Various other birds nested in small bushes or holes in stone walls, so we would visit them regularly to see how the young chicks were getting on. Sometimes we took a long road home that led us to a high hill called Kilpatrick, which had a flat top and was covered in very long heather, which was difficult to walk through. This hill has lots of history attached to it, although we did not appreciate it at the time

It was like another world where we could see all over the island including our house in the far distance, as well as most of the other houses.

We could see large ships sailing past between Rathlin and Scotland. Some of them were Cunard liners carrying passengers from Liverpool to New York and some were freight ships, inward bound from America for ports such as Glasgow, Liverpool or Belfast. Many a time I wished that I could sail with them. Watching these ships and sometimes being able to read their names, gave me a practical lesson in world geography.

Drawing by Judy McCurdy

There was still the odd sailing schooner around with its magical white sails. We could see across to the Hebridean islands and the Scottish coast fifty or more miles away, or westward to Donegal.

There were rabbits everywhere, which we chased, but they could run faster than us.

Back on the road, we would spend ages looking for wild strawberries growing in the grassy banks as they produced small but very sweet fruit.

We would pull the flowers off the wild fuschia and suck the honey from them, competing with the bees. There was an old garden near Jimmy Hegarty's house, which had belonged to the Andersons of Shandragh who had left the island. There were a lot of gooseberry bushes in it, and when they ripened in the summer we would raid them.

There were a couple of small loughs alongside the road, one of which had tiny fish called sticklebacks, and we would catch them and put them in jam jars.

Often we would see a crane or heron standing motionless on one leg waiting to catch them, with its long spring-like neck, which moved at lightning speed when a fish moved. This lough was appropriately named in Gaelic as Easc na Corr, "marsh of the crane".

Eventually I would get home to a scolding from my mother for being so late.

There was a small lough on our farm, which was about two feet deep and thirty yards wide, in a good summer it would nearly dry up. During the holidays, or after school, I sailed boats on it.

A couple of the boats were made of wood, but others were made of tin, the largest of which was made by my father from a biscuit tin. It had a sail, and I would sail it across the lough, making believe it was a real boat going to Ballycastle.

By this time we had a young cat and I would put him into the boat as a passenger, then pushing the boat out, I would run around to the other side and meet it. He would sail across the lough and jump out when it touched land and I think that he enjoyed it as he always followed me to the lough. Like all young cats he was very playful, always chasing flies, or anything that moved.

Gathering in the Harvest

The summer holidays always extended into the first two weeks of September, to allow for gathering in the harvest.

A lot of corn was sown on the island and the last week or so of August saw the start of the harvest in the lower end of the island. Being around the harbour the land was lighter, and as it was at sea level, the corn ripened earlier there.

By the first week of September, the corn had turned to a golden colour in the upper end of the island, which is heavier land and also two or three hundred feet above sea level, the barley was a darker shade than the corn.

My father used a scythe to cut the crops which had to be done on a dry day, and a good deal of skill was required to lay the sward neatly and ready for lifting. My job was to make straps for tying the sheaves which was done by taking a handful of the newly cut straw, splitting it in two, then laying the head of one on the other and twisting both together. If this was not done correctly it would pull apart. Next the strap was laid on the ground with the corn heads pointing toward the top of the sheaf, and spaced out two or three feet between them, so that the person lifting the corn could lift and tie the strap into a sheaf, almost in one movement. I was not big enough to do this until I got a few years older.

My mother helped with this, assisted by some of our neighbours, or some of the big boys of sixteen or seventeen years of age. This is where the bartering system worked when farmers would plan their work so that they could help each other out. The ancient custom of cutting the callieach was still preserved at this time. This consisted of plaiting the last couple of handfuls of corn into a three-stranded plait which was then cut and taken into the house where it was hung on the wall and kept until the next harvest. Its presence assured a good crop next year and it could not be thrown out until it was replaced by the next years callieach,. To have thrown it out earlier would have meant that a plentiful harvest was also thrown out.

After the field was cut, the next job was to make it into stooks. This was usually four or five sheaves with each side leaning against the other and it was left like this for a week or so, after which, if the weather was dry, it was carted into the stackyard near the barn, where it was built into stacks, a job which required a good deal of skill.

There were permanent circular raised stone bases, which kept the bottom of the stack from direct contact with the ground. The stack was started by standing four sheaves nearly upright at the centre. More sheaves were built against them, gradually lying flatter until the required diameter was reached, about eight or nine feet. The stack was then built up with the sides tapering outwards to cast off the rain.

When a height of about four feet was reached, the top was flat and so it was time to start tapering inwards to a point at a final height of about nine feet. The stack was then thatched with rushes to cast off the rain and securely tied with ropes, which were sometimes homemade, or else bought in coir light rope.

The homemade ropes were of straw, grass or rushes, which was twisted with a special tool called a thra hook. One person would sit on a stool beside a pile of straw, gradually feeding the straw to the person twisting the hook, who would steadily walk backwards. The completed rope was then wound into a ball or clew.

There is a Gaelic song called Casadh na Sugan, "twisting of the rope", which tells of a girl who was pestered by a fellow she did not like. One evening when he called, she got him twisting the rope, and as he backed away she opened the door which he backed out through, as soon as he was outside she jumped up, and cutting the rope with a sharp knife, slammed the door and bolted it. No doubt he got the hint!

September was the month for gathering blackberries which my mother would boil up with sugar and this went well on freshly baked bread. She would also made blackberry and redcurrant jam, as well as rhubarb and ginger jam in the spring time.

The Coming of Autumn

Autumn was taking over, the days are getting shorter with shadows getting longer, the cattle are let out on to the stubble fields to graze, there is plenty of good grass around the edges. The harvest moon is creating magical shimmering pathways across the sea, people always said that this is the brightest moon of the year, this is the time to take the fishing rod down to the rocks, and catch a couple of Lythe for the next day's dinner.

On clear frosty nights when there was no moon, myriads of stars could be seen sparkling blue and white like diamonds. The sky over Rathlin is very clear and three-dimensional, we learned the names of the various star systems at an early age. There is the Pole Star, the Plough, and the Pleiades, where legend says the first humans came from. People with very good eyesight could count eight stars in this cluster, although with a telescope, many more could be seen. When living on an island, it is important to have a knowledge of tides so we learned the phases of the moon and the tides.

Later in the winter the whole sky would be ablaze on some nights with the northern lights "Aurora Borealis". We would watch this display for ages, great beams of light in all the colours of the rainbow, red, yellow, green, flashing hundreds of miles across the sky.

The moon and tides influence the weather to a great extent. Whatever way the weather is on the day of a new or full moon, it will stay that way until the next change, such as the first quarter, or last quarter.

On a daily basis the weather will change with the tide. Very often a strong wind will get up at the first of flood tide, or alternately the wind will fall away at the start of the ebb tide. There were many natural signs which people relied on to tell what kind of weather lay ahead. Here are some which I remember.

Once the harvest was in, it was back to school for a month or so until the lifting of the potato crop.

This was the last of the field jobs, and took place from the middle to the end of October when the school would be closed, as every house would be involved in gathering in the potatoes. The potato tops had withered by this time and when the drills were split with the plough, the potatoes were flicked out into a neat row with a spade and they were left to dry. After a few hours drying in the sun and wind, they were gathered in buckets and tipped into hessian bags.

They were then carted into the stackyard and built into a pit. This was on top of the ground, and was about three feet wide at the base, tapering towards the top to about two and a half feet high, by any length, usually around twenty feet.

The pit was then thatched with either rushes or straw, and covered with a layer of soil about six inches thick to keep the frost out. A few tufts of thatch were left sticking out along the top to allow for ventilation.

The final task was to dig a trench all around the pit to carry off any rainfall, as water getting into the pit would cause the potatoes to rot.

The pits had to be kept out of reach of the cattle as they could smell the potatoes and would root with their horns and hooves to get at them. A cow could choke on a small potato, so they were only given the largest ones.

Hallowe'en and Christmas

As this marked the end of the year's fieldwork and it usually coincided with Hallowe'en, there would be a few parties around this time, with dressing up as witches, and playing games such as trick or treat. Practical jokes were also played by the older fellows, such as taking gates off houses and swapping them for other gates a good distance away. The apple fair was held in Ballycastle on the last Tuesday of October, and my father would buy a sack of apples there which would last all winter.

It was also the time to make sure that other supplies were got in before the winter. A ten stone bag of flour for bread-making, our own corn ground at the mill, coarse salt for fish curing and cooking, paraffin oil for the lamps. Coal could be bought on the island, as Neil McCuaig, who owned the pub, would bring in a couple of hundred tons each year from Ayr in Scotland. It came by puffer (small steamboat) which anchored in Church Bay, where the coal was then transferred in large sacks to Rathlin boats which brought it into the Station pier, where it was unloaded on to horse drawn carts, and taken to the old kelp store Neal McCuaig rented from Mr Gage. Islanders could buy it from here on a Friday - anything from one hundred weight to one ton. It cost about two shillings and sixpence (12p) per hundred weight loaded on to your own cart.

These were the essential basic supplies for winter. After Halloween, it was time to go back to school again and the next big event to look forward to was Christmas, which was my favourite time. For a couple of weeks before then, much of the school day was taken up with preparations for the big day.

The older pupils would be practising a play which they put on in the parochial hall, whilst everybody was involved in making decorations for the Catholic church.

We would gather ivy and bind it with heavy cord into garlands which were hung across the inside of the church by some of the men. There were two clergymen resident on the island - a Catholic priest and a Church of Ireland minister, so there were Christmas services in both Churches.

I looked forward to going to midnight mass as it was magical, with the choir singing carols and also I was allowed to stay out so late. It was the time for presents and my brother and myself were very lucky, as we had uncles and aunts in different parts of the world. My uncle George, lived in Bakersfield, California, where he was an orange grower and he would send a parcel every Christmas which contained all sorts of exotic things, such as dried fruit, raisins, sweets, American comics, and newspapers.

My mother's sister, Violet, who lived in Melbourne, Australia, did a lot of knitting with Australian wool and every year a parcel of knitted jerseys would arrive for all of us. Of course my granny, uncles and aunts in Belfast would always send us presents.

When Christmas and the New Year were over, it was time to go back to school. The days were shorter and the weather more wintry and cold at this time of year, so we did not dally on the road home. If it was raining we had various places to shelter such as behind a stone wall, in a stone quarry or an old wall stead. We knew that the best places to shelter were those where the cattle also sheltered.

Strangely enough I cannot remember many bad days, although there must have been plenty. Memory plays tricks on us. Soon after the New Year the days started to lengthen. By the start of February, there were more bright days with blue skies, which were reflected in the sea and the first day of February was regarded as the first day of Spring by the Celts.

There was a constantly changing vista of the distant hills of Ireland and Scotland, which were blue, and at times land would appear to rise out of the sea. At other times it could not be seen. I think that is what gave rise to the story of The Enchanted Island.

The next big event to look forward to was Easter which was the time for Easter eggs. My relatives in Belfast would send me a chocolate one and we would hard boil eggs in whin (gorse) blossom which would turn them to a golden colour. I was often given duck eggs or goose eggs for this and we would have a competition rolling them down a hill and the egg which lasted longest was the winner. Sometimes we would eat them after they were broken.

Cattle Dealers

Cattle dealers would come to the island a couple of times a year, in the Springtime and the Autumn and they would go around looking at any young cattle that might be for sale. As Rathlin animals were always in demand, dealers would try to outdo each other by coming in earlier than expected. Farmers would usually have their favourite dealer, and refuse to sell to another one.

My father always dealt with Joe Donnelly from Ballycastle and I can remember listening to them haggling over the price of an animal. The prices were not great in the 1930s, a two year old beast would fetch six or seven pounds at best, however the price of two or three would pay a lot of the bills for a year. When a price was agreed, the dealer would pay in cash and there were usually a few of the large white five pound notes, as well as maybe a couple of one pound or ten shilling notes and a few half crowns. The reason for the smaller notes and silver change had to do with an old tradition known as the 'Luck Penny'. When an animal was sold and paid for, it was the custom to give back a small part of the price for luck, and so the dealer would always make sure that the farmer could not use the excuse of having no small notes nor change.

The animal bought, had then to be boated out of the island at the first suitable opportunity. This was always done at the seller's risk. If anything happened to the animal, the seller was responsible, so arrangements were made with a boat to ship the cattle out on a good calm day. As others would be doing the same thing, a boat might do two or three trips in one day.

The cattle were driven along the road to the pier where they were herded together and then thrown on their side on a pile of straw or bracken. Their feet were tied and they were slid into the boat onto another bed of straw where they would lie comfortably on the journey to Ballycastle. When they were untied and released on to the pier sometimes they would take off at a gallop, however, with everyone in pursuit, they were soon captured before getting into the town centre. Young fellows would test out their running skills by getting in front of the animal and then they would (cap it) turn it back.

When the cattle were sold, it was time to settle up bills with traders in Ballycastle which was the custom and was done a couple of times a year. During the year, islanders would order supplies from such as the grocer, coal merchant, timber merchant, chemist, vet, and the hardware shop, this was always done on the understanding that the bills would be settled in Spring and Autumn.

There was always a great deal of trust between Ballycastle traders and islanders as they knew each for generations.

Winter Nights and Social Activities

Winter nights were for sitting around the fire. After my father milked the cows and fed them, we would have our tea - often a boiled egg with bread and butter. We sat around the fire and as there was no electricity for light, we used a couple of oil lamps which burned paraffin oil. My mother often knitted socks or sewed a patch on something such as my trousers, while sometimes a neighbour would call in. We had a gramophone and a good supply of records, sent to us by my aunt and uncle in Belfast, and they were very popular in the winter time. There was always plenty of social activity on the island, especially in the winter evenings and one popular pastime was to visit each others houses, known as 'going for a ceili'.

Ceili is a Gaelic word, which translates to 'evening visit' and this is what it was. After the work was done, the cows milked and fed and everyone had their tea, at about nine o'clock it was time to go for a ceili to a neighbour's house.

As there was no television in those days, most houses had a wireless or radio, working on a wet battery, which had to be sent to Ballycastle for re-charging every few weeks, as there was no electricity supply on the island. For this reason the wireless was only switched on to listen to the news or traditional music from

Radio Eireann. There was always card playing before Christmas, usually for a goose or a rooster and twenty-five would have been the usual game, whist drives would be organised in the parish hall.

Conversation was about farming, fishing and the weather, with a bit of story telling later in the evening. Often these tales were about something that had happened to someone in the past few weeks and they were often very funny. There was always someone who was the butt of a joke and if they were present they had to make the best of it.

There were a couple of houses we visited regularly in the winter, one of these houses was known as Glac an ti Mor (the big house in the hollow), the last house on the road west, and the home of Daniel and Mary Ann Mc Faul, who lived there with their family, Dan, Neil, James, Johnny, Lily and Rosie and grandson Brendan. It was the last stopping place for lighthouse keepers on their way to the West Lighthouse. They would stop for a cup of tea and a bottle of fresh milk to take back with them. Coming from the "lower end" harbour area, or even the pub, they would always have the latest island or Ballycastle news, stories and gossip, with which they would entertain everyone for a while. They would then continue their journey along the last lonely mile to the lighthouse. One or two of them had motor bikes and those who had push bikes found it hard work on the rough hilly roads.

Other stories would be told of people and times now gone and some of the old men had a gift for telling stories which were translated from the Gaelic. There was the odd ghost story as the night wore on, which was told for the benefit of young ones like myself. We would pretend not to listen, but we were taking it all in, and then would be afraid to walk home.

The woman of the house would always make a cup of tea for the visitors, who would always say "ah sure you shouldn't have bothered", to which she would reply "sure it's only a drop in your hand". The tea was usually accompanied by a plateful of soda bread, with butter and jam and soon after this it would be

Seamus McCurdy playing an accordion, c. 1930s
Courtesy of Gabrielle McCurdy

time to go home. When we were leaving, Mrs Mary Ann McFaul would come out to the gate with us. This was her opportunity to tell my mother some gossip which she couldn't find the chance to tell when the men were sitting around listening, and we would stand there for ten minutes or so. Then we would start to walk on, Mary Ann walking with us, passing a couple of other houses, before she decided that she had gone far enough. By this time I was half asleep and my father had to carry me over his shoulder.

Another ceili house was the home of James and Cassie "John Beag" McCurdy in South Cleggan. Cassie was related to my father on the Anderson side. They lived there with their family, Sean, Seamus, Joey, Michael, Brigid, Mary and Lily, there had been another one Patrick, who had died as a child.

James and his son Seamus could play the accordion, and Joey, Lily and Seamus were good singers. There was always good fun as well as songs and music and like McFauls, lighthouse keepers called in with the latest stories and gossip.

Sean was the eldest of the family. He was very good at woodwork and was always making something in his workshop, I liked going there to watch him and learn. Joey was younger and full of devilment. Unfortunately, it was he who fell over a cliff and was killed.

Ghosts and Fairies

There were a couple of places on the road, which I was always afraid of passing, as they were supposed to be haunted by ghosts and fairies.

The first place was a dark glen Bealach an Rani (the road of the ferns) where a woman had once seen a fairy band, they were the size of small children and dressed in red and green suits, sitting on a heathery bank playing music. Different people said that they had seen them. The place was named Bealach an Sluaigh, "the road of the fairies."

Another place which I found to be scary was near to the site of an old school, Pairc an Tigh Scoile, "the field of the schoolhouse". It was in a deep glen named An Fallt "the glen".

A man who was a neighbour of ours had a strange experience when he was walking home one night at this place. He met another man whom he recognised as one who had died a month earlier, and the ghost said to him that he had been bidden to come back and settle an unpaid debt. He asked our neighbour if he would help him to complete his business and the man agreed, but he would never talk to anyone about it, other than to say that it involved going to Belfast.

There were other places where strange things were believed to happen. Doige was a dark glen where a big black dog was supposed to live which would attack people walking on the road at night. There was also another strange creature at this place which was called the Sac Ban. It was wrapped in a white sack and would roll along the road following people.

The most fearsome creature was the Ceannan Dubh "Black Horse with white forehead mark" which was always around after dark, galloping at high speed. It carried a spear attached to its chest, and when it attacked a person they would not survive, it spread terror amongst the people.

One evening a woman was returning to her own house after a visit to a neighbour. As it was getting dark she took a short cut across a wide reach of mountain. Soon she heard galloping hooves and nearly fainted. She started to run, fear lending wings to her feet, but just as the horse was almost upon her, she managed with superhuman effort to leap over a high stone wall. The last sound she heard before fainting, was an unearthly piercing scream. Her family found her still in a faint, from which she soon recovered, but the sight which brought great joy to everyone was the dead body of the horse lying extended on the heather. It had run at full speed into the wall and the spear was driven back through its heart killing it. There was great rejoicing after this as the threat was gone, yet, oddly enough, one or two horses are still seen by some people, whilst they remain invisible to others who are with them.

There is a story associated with our own house. My grandfather Joseph had four brothers who all emigrated to

Scotland in the 1850s, finding employment in the Clyde shipyards. One of them, John, went to sea in a sailing clipper bound for Argentina.

Before he left Rathlin he was building a new barn, which he left unfinished, so my grandfather finished it off and put on the thatched roof (his father had died young). As was the custom, he invited the neighbours for a ceili in celebration of the new barn.

As the evening wore on, my grandfather went outside to have a look at the barn in the moonlight. He got quite a shock, as standing there by the barn was his brother, John, dressed, as he said, in a long American coat. At first my grandfather thought that John had arrived as a surprise for them, but as he called out to the rest of the people in the house and moved to greet his brother, the apparition faded away.

There was much debate about the meaning of this, but my grandfather knew instinctively that it meant bad news. Something was wrong and sure enough, a few weeks later, a letter arrived to say that there had been a collision in the River Plate, near Uruguay, and John had been drowned. So far as we know he was buried there. The walls of that barn are still standing.

Story Tellers

There were some good story tellers on the island, one of the best being Donal Eoin Ruadh McCurdy, who lived in North Kinraver and although he was before my time, I feel that I know him, as his name was mentioned so often in connection with certain stories. I have managed to collect some of his stories as follows.

The Mermaid

There was a man in North Cleggan, in the upper end of the island, who was down at the shore one day gathering sticks for the fire when he saw a mermaid and she had her cloak off. He managed to get hold of the cloak before she could reach it and so she had to follow him home. He hid the cloak in the thatch where she could not find it and anyhow it seems that she was happy enough there and settled down to a life on the land. They had a family who looked just as normal as anyone else.

One day the man was in Ballycastle at the Lammas Fair and there came on a bit of a storm and he was not able to get back until the next day. After landing in O'Berne port and hauling the boat up, he headed off home to North Cleggan where a sorry sight met him. His two children were in tears as their mother had gone, and a neighbour woman was looking after them. During the storm a bit of the thatch had started to blow off and when she went out to fix it she found her cloak. As soon as she put it on, an urge to return to the sea came over her. Of course the man went to look for her, but she had disappeared and was never seen again, so he reared the children on his own, and people said that you would not know any difference between them and any others except that they had very flat feet.

The Enchanted Island

There is an enchanted island, which rises out of the sea every seven years and it was said that if you picked up some soil from under your foot and managed to throw it onto the island, it would stay above the sea forever.

At this time, there were two hiring fairs held in Ballycastle, one was in May and the other in November.

There was a girl from Rathlin at the fair and she was hired by a farmer. Soon, they left the fair in a horse drawn trap heading to his home, as they got outside the town and on to the open road, he put a hood over her head and told her not to be afraid. When they got to his house he took the hood off and she had no idea where she was. She did all the jobs she was given and the farmer looked after her very well.

When the six months were up, the farmer paid her wages and told her to get ready for the journey back to Ballycastle. As they left the house, he put the hood on her head again, well, as they were arriving back in the town, he took the hood off her, telling her that she must never try to tell anyone where she had been, and that if she ever saw him at the fair again she was not to speak to him. When they arrived back in Ballycastle, she made her way to the pier to catch a boat for Rathlin. On arriving home she could not tell anyone where she had been as she had no memory of it.

Sometime later she was again in Ballycastle at the hiring fair, and who did she see but the farmer she had been hired with, although he had warned her not to speak to him if she saw him at the fair, she thought that it would be very ill mannered of her to ignore him, so she ran over to speak to him, He re-acted very angrily and gave her a switch of a coat he had over his shoulder which blinded her for a time and when she recovered, the farmer had vanished. People who had seen said that he was from the enchanted island, and that is where she had been hired. On returning to Rathlin, she never went near the hiring fair again, and although she lived to a great age, she still could not recall where she had been hired.

Finn Mc Cool Visits Rathlin

The giant, Finn McCool, came on a visit to Rathlin to hunt hares and he brought his son Oisin, who was about twelve years old at the time, and who was to undergo the first of his tests before he could join the Fianna, a warrior band who went everywhere with Finn. He also brought his faithful dog Bran, a large Irish wolfhound, who could run so fast that the ground caught fire under his paws.

They also brought nine hares in baskets. On landing their boats in the old port of O'Berne they set out to find a five acre field to set up the test for Oisin, which was to keep the nine hares in the field, none were to escape

The only suitable field of this size in this part of the island was in Garvagh, so they released the nine hares from their baskets, and they ran in all directions. Oisin could run faster and no matter which way they went he was in front of them. After a time the hares got tired, they knew that they couldn't get away from him, so they sat down in a circle in the middle of the field, and they were put back into their baskets, Oisin had passed the test.

The Fianna then set off to hunt Rathlin hares, above Killeany cliffs they raised a few in the long grass and bracken. The hares set off at high speed up the hill, running so fast that even Bran could not keep up with them, on they went past Carn na Seile, after which the ground was flatter and Bran began to catch up with them, but then, up they went over the mountain until they reached the ancient fort Dun Mor, by which time Bran was close behind them, when suddenly a cave opened up in the side of Dun Mor and they disappeared inside with Bran after them. The hill closed over them and Finn, Oisin and the Fianna were just in time to see what had happened, they could not believe what they had just seen. Finn was distraught at losing his dog Bran.

Approaching the hill carefully, the gap in the hill opened up again, Finn, Oisin and his warriors entered and found themselves in a large cavern which closed behind them, they were transported in an instant to Tir na n'Og, the land of youth, where they were told that the hares which they had hunted were in reality Rathlin people from Tir na n'Og, who were allowed to return to earth on one day per year, Finn and his companions were told that if they stayed for more than three days, they could never return.

Finn decided that although Tir na n'Og was the most beautiful place that he had ever seen, he could not stay, so he and the Fianna returned to Rathlin. Oisin was so enchanted with the place that he wanted to stay a while longer, so Finn agreed, but as we know, Oisin overstayed the three days, and it was nine hundred years later when he was allowed to return on horseback. He was warned not to set foot on the land at his peril.

Galloping along on his white horse at the speed of the wind, he came upon some men who were trying to move a large stone and being immensely strong he stopped to help them. As he put one hand to the stone and moved it, the girth of his saddle broke and Oisin fell to the ground. Immediately he turned into a very old man and died on that spot.

Gaelic

During my childhood, Gaelic was still commonly used in conversation, particularly in the upper end of the island. The Gaelic of Rathlin was a mixture of Scots and Irish which reflected the mix of the population.

My father was a fluent speaker, but having studied in Donegal, he had a lot of Donegal Irish. Although Gaelic was widely understood, there were a few families who had none.

Almost all of the place names are Irish in origin and they describe the land, whether it is a high or a low field. Crop growing, hills, cliffs, streams, valleys, wet lands, headlands, everything has a name, and many are still in use. Fortunately most of these names have been recorded in a Rathlin place names book, which includes maps of their locations.

The language gradually declined, due in part to lengthy periods in the school when there was no teacher of Gaelic and emigration also contributed to this loss.

Some names in our Townland of Ballygill South

Garbhach-	the rough field
An Glaic Fluich-	the wet hollow
Lag na Beinne-	the hollow at the cliff
Glaic an Toigh Allais-	the sweat house
Beinne Mor-	the big cliff
Glaic an Acair-	the hollow of the acre
Lag an Fada-	the long hollow
An Garradh Mor-	the big garden
Pairc an Toighe Scoile-	the field of the school

An Pairc Beag-	the small field
Bord an Fhallt-	the top of the glen
An Creagan Buidhe-	the yellow rocky place
Cathaor an Mhuiller-	the chair of the miller

Gaelic Words in Everyday Use

The English dialect which was spoken on Rathlin, contained a number of words which were Gaelic in origin, although often the speaker was unaware of the Gaelic root of the word. Unfortunately, modern influences have eradicated much of this colourful vernacular speech. Here is a small selection of words which I can recall.

Bruach	Slope or Brae.
Bool	Pot Hook for Crane.
Cap	Stop or Turn Animals.
Clabber	Muck, Gutters.
Clic	Hook
Chee Chee	Call for Cows
Jook	Peep or Hide Around Corner or Door
Gullion	Wet or Boggy Ground
Fornenst	In Front of You
Glar	Deep Sticky Mud
Gob	Mouth, Beak
Gulpan	Fool, Idiot
Langle	Fetter an Animal's Feet
Scobe	Bite off bits of a Turnip
Spags	Feet
Slap	Gap in a Wall
Sheugh	Shallow Trench or Drain
Stoor	Dust
Sprahal	Struggle from Tripping
Teeming	Heavy Rain
Tovey	Boaster
Wheen	More Than a Few, Less Than a Lot.

SUNDAYS

Sunday was a day for going to Church, recreation and visiting.

The only work done that day was milking and feeding the cows in the morning and evening. In the Catholic Church, or Chapel, as it was generally called, there were two masses said, the first one being at half past eight, and the second at eleven in the morning. The majority of people went to the second one and, incidentally, I have since learned that only the Anglican or Church of Ireland faith was allowed to use the title Church, hence Catholic Churches were given the lesser title of Chapel.

The church of St Thomas, Anglican or Church of Ireland, held a service at eleven in the morning.

Everyone dressed up to attend Church when men wore blue or black suits with a shirt and tie, and well polished boots. Most of the men had a pair of fine boots, which they only wore on Sundays, or at weddings and funerals.

Women also dressed up in their finest. The younger ones wore a costume complete with a hat and the older women wore a long black skirt nearly down to the ground, with a black blouse and sometimes a black shawl around their shoulders and of course a hat. In the Church, the women always sat on the left hand seats and the men on the right, thus they were completely segregated. At the back, there were always a few who came in late and would sit on the floor, or kneel on one knee. They could be heard gossiping and giggling. I have since seen this in other rural parts of Ireland, and indeed it is still done today by people who are in their seventies and old enough to have grown up.

Before the mass started, the men would all stay outside leaning or sitting on the stone wall, whilst exchanging news and views or gossiping. The men from the upper end of the island always stayed on the upper side of the church gate, and the lower end men on the lower side of the gate.

There was very little mixing of the two groups and after the mass was over, they would gather again outside to continue the gossip, sometimes for up to half an hour.

Some were experts at creating an argument. I remember two men, one of them related to me and the other his close neighbour, who would pretend to argue over whatever the priest had said in his sermon. They always appeared to be deadly serious, and others who were listening to what was said would soon join in. Within a few minutes voices were raised as theological matters were debated and I can remember the priest coming out of the vestry to see what the row was about. Of course by this time the two who had started it had left to go home. It was amazing how some fell into the trap every time.

Gradually everybody would drift off to walk several miles home as then there were no motor cars on the island. There might be two or three who would bring a horse and trap, especially for the elderly people.

Walking was no bother to people then. We lived two miles from the Church and we would walk home after mass. In the summer, if there was a model yacht race in Ushet Lough, I and sometimes my father, if he was free, would walk the four miles to the lough and after the race walk the same distance home again. On other days there might be a football match in the evening and from the age of ten I was involved in the upper end team, which had all ages from myself to grown men. I would walk a couple of miles or more to the match, and then after it was over I would walk or run home again. On some Sundays I would cover twelve or fourteen miles on rough gravel roads without tarmac.

There was a lighthouse keeper Mickey Doherty, who was very good at football, and he would train us before a match against the lower end team. He also showed myself and a few of the other youngsters how to put a man off the ball. The idea was to run alongside your opponent for a few steps, then knock his knee with your own, which would cause him to trip and fall as his knees knocked together. I carried out this trick against a few of the grown men and it always worked, as I was able to get away with the ball. I could run pretty fast, and I needed to, as they got up again and threatened to kill me if they got hold of me. Nowadays this would be classed as a professional foul and would probably get a red card. There was a great deal of rivalry between the two ends of the island.

Yacht Races and Dances

Model yacht racing was a traditional pastime on the island where it had been going on for generations. In earlier times the yachts had been fairly large, up to four feet long, and with masts about six feet high. In my childhood these larger yachts were going out of fashion, and smaller ones about two or two and a half feet long, and with masts no more than four feet high were becoming common. They were made out of a solid block of wood, shaped by hand and hollowed out to make them lighter. They had a deep keel, with up to seven pounds of lead fixed to it.

The races took place on bank holidays throughout the summer, starting with Easter. there were no races in the winter.

The main venue was Ushet Lough in the lower end of the island and Cleggan Lough in the upper end was also used. Cleggan was a more difficult venue as it was surrounded by hills and rarely did the wind blow directly on it, consequently there were always eddies or squalls which made sailing more erratic.

Each competitor paid an entrance fee and there was a cup for the winner as well as a small cash prize. Second and third places would also receive cash prizes.

The start and finish were between two sets of flags and anywhere outside of these did not count. The positions of the flags was decided on race day according to the wind direction. The first leg was against the wind and the second with it, with the third and final leg against the wind. The real skill was in setting the sails, particularly to get a yacht to sail directly into the wind. The sails which were used were known as Bermuda rig, which consisted of a mainsail fixed to the mast and a boom. A jib was fixed to the mast and a bowsprit, which extended out over the bow of the yacht. When running with the wind, a square sail would be used, or alternately the main sail was set square against the mast, which was known as sailing goose wings.

There was serious competition, and of course there was a set of rules, which were enforced by a race committee. A yacht could be picked up and carried if it ran in on a lee shore, but if it ran in on a windward shore, it had to be sailed out of it. At times someone who was trying to be crafty would pick up and carry their yacht on a windward shore, but if caught doing this they would be disqualified, and then the arguments would begin.

There was usually a dance held in the parochial hall in the evening where prizes would be distributed for the races.

Regatta and Sports Day

There was a regatta held every year in July and the boats which took part were twenty or twenty-two foot fishing boats. There were sailing races and rowing races and boats came in from Ballycastle, Ballintoy and Dunseverick, so the competition was tough, but the island crews could hold their own against all comers.

Preparations started in the Spring when sails were got ready and as the boats carried the maximum sail, everything had to be checked and tested, or new sails made before the big day.

These boats usually had one mast, but on race day, the main mast was moved back to roughly the middle of the boat and this carried the large main sail. A second smaller mast was fixed forward of this to carry a foresail and a jib which was attached to a bowsprit.

Preparation for the rowing races was just as keen, masts and anything else which wasn't needed was removed to lighten the boat. Crews would practise rowing at speed, but they usually did this in one of the secluded bays out of sight of other crews, as they were not going to give away their tactics. It was necessary to have tough hands, but this was no problem for Rathlin men as they were used to rowing. For someone who was new to it, or had not rowed for a good while, their hands were soft, and they would soon get blisters, which made it impossible to row.

As these were all working boats, they were always in the water during the fishing season, and they absorbed a good deal of water. In order to lighten them, they would be hauled out of the water, if possible for a few days before the races, and left to dry out, losing a good bit of weight. Of course if they dried out too much, they would start leaking water through any cracks which opened up.

The regatta took place in the morning over a course set out in Church Bay, and just as in modern yacht racing, tactics were all important, particularly rounding a buoy. It was not unknown for a boat to try to sneak on the inside of the buoy but if they were spotted they were reported to the regatta committee, and occasionally were disqualified. Being tough fishermen they did not take kindly to disqualification. The best view of the races was from the cliffs above the bay, where I would sit with my father.

The regatta was followed by sports in the afternoon, which were held in a field belonging to Neal McCuaig, the publican. There were always a lot of visitors from Ballycastle and the surrounding area for these events. There was a full range of athletic events and competition was tough, but the highlights were a football match and a tug-of-war. An island team would be fielded in each of these events and having practised and trained for months beforehand, they were usually too good for the visitors. Sometimes the visitors won and there was an occasion when a visiting football team beat the island team and later in the evening the visitors went to the pub to celebrate the event. The landlord locked the door and refused entry to them because they had the nerve to beat an island team!

To finish off the day, there was always a dance in the parochial hall in the evening when Rathlin musicians usually supplied the music. Occasionally a visiting musician would come for the event, usually an accordion or fiddle player.

There would be a good few Scottish visitors on holiday during what was known as the Glasgow Fair, they were visiting relatives on the island, so there was a great variety of dances, both Scottish and Irish. Of course there was The Lancers, a traditional Rathlin dance, which is a five-part, eight hand set lasting for about ten minutes so the dancers had to be fit. Other dances were the six-hand reel, Siege of Ennis, Walls of Limerick, Pride of Erin Waltz, Waves of Tory and many more. To give the dancers a break, tea and sandwiches were served midway through the evening and there were always a few good singers in the hall, such as Paddy and John Black, Alec McCurdy, Seamus, Joey and Lily McCurdy who could be persuaded to give a song or two. Some songs I remember being sung were, Fare Thee Well Enniskillen, Rose of Mooncoin, Dark Island, Red River Valley, and Rose of Aranmore. There was always a good range of songs, after which the dancing would start up again, going on until the early hours.

When the dance finished around 2 am or later, some of the mainland boats would be going home, so visitors would get a lift with them, Of course it was daylight from 3am and the weather was usually good. The regatta and sports day was the highlight of the year.

Rathlin fishermen would go home and change into their working clothes, then go straight out to lift the long lines or lobster creels, without any sleep, but they were used to this hectic life style in the summer time. As soon as they had delivered their catch to Ballycastle, they came back home to start a day's work on the farm.

Rathlin sailing regatta 1926 (boat Ida).
John McCurdy, Crockaharnan at helm, James McCurdy, Cleggan,
brother of John, Johnnie Curry, Ballynoe, Paddy Anderson,
the Station.

My father in Uniform, c 1916

Ships sailing in convoy through Rathlin Sound, World War Two.
Courtesy of L. McQuilkin

HMS Drake dressed overall with flags.

HMS Drake sinking in Church Bay, Rathlin

Weddings, Wakes and Funerals

A wedding was always a big occasion on Rathlin as all the neighbours were invited. After the wedding service, there was the wedding breakfast, which was always at the bride's home and this would be for family and relatives. After this a box camera would be produced and photos were taken. In the evening the real festivities would get under way in earnest, musicians would strike up and the dancing would get started.

There was always a drink - whiskey or porter for the men and the older women might also try a drop of something stronger than tea. For the young ones there was tea, lemonade or fizzy soda. Plenty of stories and yarns were told as the night progressed and then various singers would give a song. My father was always in demand, as he was a good singer.

Another important event was a death. The traditional wake would take place for one or two days after the death. Islanders would visit the home of the deceased to pay their respects, staying for a couple of hours. They were always offered a cup of tea and something to eat. Evening visiting was most common and the older men would be offered tobacco if they smoked, as most did. There would also be a small glass of whiskey, Uisce Beatha or (water of life) as it is translated from the Gaelic. A few neighbours would take it in turns to stay the night so that the relatives were not left on their own.

On the day of the funeral, islanders would gather at the house. The coffin would be carried by the men on their shoulders, four at a time, changing over constantly until they reached the Church. After the Requiem, they continued to the island graveyard, where a few prayers were said, after which neighbours would return to the house of the deceased for a chat and a cup of tea. This burial ground has been in use for hundreds of years by all denominations.

Boat Engines and Model Railways

I particularly remember the Minister, Rev. Brown, who had been an engineer before taking up Holy Orders.

He built a model railway, which ran around his garden and sometimes he would invite children from the school to see it working.

He was good at everything mechanical. In Ballymena he would buy second hand engines, mainly from Austin Seven cars, and fit them into boats on the island. They had a limited life, as they were cooled with salt water, for which they were not designed.

Another job, which he did, was to generate the very first electricity on the island. He used a stream which ran down past the priest's house and the Catholic Church. First he built a concrete dam in the stream to store the water, then he installed a waterwheel which operated a turbine, thus generating electricity. He wired up the priest's house and connected this to the turbine, so this was the first house on the island to have electric light. Unfortunately he was unable to do the same in his own house, as there were no streams nearby.

The system at the priest's house worked well in the wintertime, but in the summertime when there was a shortage of rainfall, the stream would nearly dry up, and so the waterwheel could not turn.

Shipwrecks

Over the centuries there were many shipwrecks on Rathlin and most of these were sailing ships, either outward bound for America, or inward bound for Belfast or Liverpool.

I can remember hearing my father talking with others such as Mickey Joe Anderson or James (John Beag) McCurdy about these wrecks. One was the *Girvan* of Ayr, a sailing barque which was outward bound from Glasgow to Melbourne.

She ran aground on Clachan Bo near Bull Point, at the western end of the island. It seems that due to the lack of wind the tide carried her onto the reef. Being loaded with a general cargo of farming equipment, such as ploughs, anvils etc. plus 500 cases of whiskey which was soon "liberated" by the islanders. Boats even came from the mainland to help with the "liberation". The whiskey was in great demand and I have seen furniture such as tables which came from the *Girvan*.

There were a few ships torpedoed by German submarines during the first world war. One was the *Knights Gareth* which was torpedoed to the west of Rathlin. The crew abandoned ship and managed to get ashore near the Giant's Causeway and the ship drifted ashore near a place called Tollabhae Cave at the west end of the island. There were plenty of supplies aboard which islanders found very useful. Another ship which was wrecked in the same place, was the *Bouncer* which was a salvage ship sent to salvage the *Knights Gareth* in 1921. The work was going well and the weather was good, so the crew decided to go to a ceili on the island, but during the night a heavy sea got up, and when the crew returned, they found that their ship had been driven ashore and was a total wreck. History does not tell us what was said by the crew or the owners, but I imagine that it was not the sort of language which would be heard in Church.

Another ship which met its end on Rathlin was HMS *Drake*, a large 14,000 ton cruiser, which was torpedoed by a German submarine on 2 October 1917. The ship had been hit north of Rathlin, and in an attempt to make it to Church Bay with damaged steering gear, she rammed another ship, the *Mendip Range*, which made it to Ballycastle Bay and was beached. The *Drake* capsized in Church Bay, Rathlin and is marked by a buoy. It was ironic that the ship which was named after Francis Drake, who had wrought havoc on Rathlin in an earlier time, should meet its end on Rathlin. When I was a youngster the side could be seen at low tide lying like a great whale. It has since become a good fishing spot for Lythe and Conger eels.

The same submarine also torpedoed another ship the *Lugano* between Rathlin and Ballintoy. The destroyer HMS *Brisk* was also sunk close to the same place as the *Lugano*, so the German submarine was responsible for the destruction of four ships in one day.

A lighthouse was constructed on the cliffs at Bull Point between 1912 and 1917, and came into service after the First World War ended. This, together with the end of sail, and the use of more reliable engines reduced the number of ships running ashore.

On the 1 March 1930 a Fleetwood trawler *Shackleton* came ashore in thick fog at a place called Greenan Point on the north coast of Rathlin. There was thick fog and it was dark.

The Rathlin life-saving crew under the leadership of Joseph Anderson (Mickey Joe's father) made their way to the cliff, having to carry their equipment over rough mountainous territory. Arriving there, the next problem was to get a line across the wreck in the fog and darkness. Guided by the shouts of the crew, they succeeded on the sixth attempt. Having secured a rope on the ship, the breeches buoy equipment was set up. This was a lifebelt apparatus attached to running ropes and the crewmen were winched one at a time through the water to the shore and then up a two hundred cliff to safety.

Some island men had to climb half way down the cliff to a ledge to release the sailors from the breeches buoy and then once free they were taken up a rope ladder to the cliff top. The rescue continued through the night until 6am, the next morning, when all fourteen crew men were rescued. As they were soaking wet and cold, they were taken to houses in Ballygill, Brockley, Glacklugh, Garvagh, Cleggan and Glackanacre and given food and dry clothing by the islanders and I remember my father saying that two were brought to our house.

The crew were taken off the island the next day by another Fleetwood trawler which was in the vicinity.

The only means of communication with the outside world was via the Post Office wireless transmitter, and so the postmistress, Ms Mary Anderson, kept the Post Office open all night to deal with transmissions. In a way this was appropriate, as it was from Rathlin, that the world's first commercial wireless transmissions were made by Marconi thirty-two years before, in 1898.

The island life-saving crew was awarded the National Life-Saving Shield as well as a presentation from the trawler owners and a marble tablet inscribed with all of their names which was erected in the Parochial Hall.

The next ship to run on the rocks was the *Hinde,* a Dutch coaster, on 17 March 1940, again in thick fog, but this time the crew of eight were able to get ashore so they made their way to the West Lighthouse and raised the alarm. My father was the only one on duty when a Dutch sailor made an appearance. His English was limited and my father said that he announced that there was a "sheep on rocks", You can imagine my father's surprise when this man appeared, as the "sheep" was no more than a mile from the lighthouse with its light and foghorn blasting out!

The *Hinde* was carrying a load of seed potatoes from Derry and some were afterwards used as seed on the island.

The next wreck was the *Lough Garry* on the night of 20 January 1942 which sank half a mile from the shore on the East side of the island. As it was a dark night and snowing, with gale force winds blowing, by the time the islanders discovered the wreck, twenty nine men had lost their lives.

After the *Drake* had sunk there was cordite, used for firing guns, washed ashore from it for many years. As youngsters we used to gather it off the shore and if a piece was lit it would fizzle away. We would pack it tightly into a can or metal fishing float leaving one piece sticking out as a fuse. We would then light this and run away and hide behind a wall to await an almighty explosion and bits of shrapnel flying through the air. It's a wonder we survived. Another thing which we did was to set off magnesium flares which were washed ashore in boxes in the early years of the war. These were designed to be used in a special flare gun, but we did not have one, so we would put them into a piece of metal drainpipe and hit the cap with a large nail and a stone. I can remember we did this one night and it attracted the attention of the police in Ballycastle, who came over in a boat to investigate, but of course by the time they got here we had all disappeared. Such were our pastimes.

Rathlin and the Second World War

A day, which has always stayed in my memory, is Sunday 3 September 1939. That was the day we heard that Britain and France had declared war on Germany. To us children it brought a sense of foreboding, we did not really know what it meant.

The event was heralded by a violent thunderstorm on Rathlin, so maybe the gods of war were having their say!

My father certainly knew what it meant, as twenty one years previously, he had seen the end of World War One, in which he spent four years on the battlefields of France and Belgium.

As a young man he had left Rathlin, after his studies at the Gaelic College, to go to Greenock in Scotland where he had three uncles living, as well as cousins who were teaching there.

His idea was to get a job and possibly to get into teaching, however, this was when World War One had just started, and he, like thousands of other young men was caught up in the euphoria of the slogan "Your Country Needs You".

The general impression created was that it was all a great adventure, and if they joined the army, they would get a uniform, free food and accommodation, as well as good pay and it would all be over in a few months, when they would return to a land "fit for heroes".

The reality turned out to be very different as this was no holiday in the vineyards of France. There was unbelievable hardship, living in mud and water in the trenches, with death all around and poor quality tinned food and not enough of it.

I can remember my father saying that the first fresh bread they saw in three years was when the American Army arrived and set up field kitchens and bakeries. The British army generals had no respect for human life and were incompetent.

Gullible boys went to the battlefields of France, and those who were lucky enough to return, were old men before their time, with their health destroyed by poison gas and mustard gas. The land fit for heroes did not materialise, instead it became a land of unemployment and poverty for many.

Some aspects of the Second World War came close to Rathlin, Very large convoys of ships would pass on the north side of the island, inbound from the USA and Canada heading for Liverpool and Glasgow with supplies of every sort.

They soon attracted the attention of German submarines and warplanes. The submarines lay in wait in the seaway approaching Malin Head and Islay and many ships were sunk in this area.

German planes started to bomb the convoys and as a result of this most ships began to carry large amounts of timber as deck cargo. This provided protection in the event of being bombed. I can recall seeing ships burning after a bombing raid.

The timber was most often in the form of small tree trunks about six or eight feet long and were needed as pit props in the coalmines in Britain, however, in the event of the ship being sunk all of this timber would float off. At times the seas around Rathlin were full of such timber. I remember hearing a boatman say that there was one day when he could almost have walked to Ballycastle on floating timber.

Of course much of this was washed up on Rathlin and made good firewood or fencing posts. There were also much larger logs came ashore which were claimed by the Customs and Excise and the finders were offered a small reward.

The convoys were protected to some extent by naval ships, such as destroyers or corvettes which would race around at high speed, and if they detected the sound of a submarine engine, they would start to depth charge the area.

I recall one day when I was out fishing in the South Cleggan boat off Bull Point, with James, Sean, Joey and Michael McCurdy, when we heard the sound of explosions and knew immediately what it was. Very soon we saw a destroyer heading in our direction firing depth charges, so we quickly started up our Austin Seven engine and headed for safety at full speed, which was about five or six miles per hour. Small fishing boats had to be constantly on the alert for such hazards and they were not allowed to fish after dusk.

Magnetic mines were another danger as they were designed to stick to an iron ship and explode. As the war progressed, copper bands fixed at waterline level protected many ships. Some of these large mines were washed up on Rathlin and had to be reported by the Rathlin Coastguard and naval experts would come in and neutralise them.

There were always a lot of planes around. Spitfires and Hurricanes practised low flying over the island and often they were not much higher than the chimneys. There was a headland called Sron Deargan (red nose) near where we lived which they used for target practice using dummy ammunition. Sometimes us youngsters would gather up the empty machine gun bullet cases.

Other planes around were Sunderlands, Catalina flying boats, and Wellington bombers.

There was one occasion when the island was used by military forces for a mock invasion, which was a practice for eventual landings in France.

Apart from this, life continued as normal on Rathlin, but for me there was an unforeseen shock in store. My idyllic life came to an abrupt end when my father died in 1942, partly due to health problems incurred in the First World War.

This event was to lead to myself and my mother and brother going to live in Belfast which started a new chapter in my life. It opened my eyes to the reality of life in Northern Ireland.